OLD ILLINOIS HOUSES

OLD ILLINOIS HOUSES

by

JOHN DRURY

THE UNIVERSITY OF CHICAGO PRESS
Chicago and London

Dedicated

to my wife

MARION NEVILLE

and to our Irish terrier,

Fedelma the Ruddy,

both of whom toured Illinois with me

in the preparation of this book.

THE UNIVERSITY OF CHICAGO PRESS, CHICAGO 60637
THE UNIVERSITY OF CHICAGO PRESS, LTD., LONDON

Copyright 1941 by the Chicago Daily News
Published 1948 by the Illinois State Historical Society
All rights reserved. Reprinted 1977
Printed in the United States of America
81 80 79 78 77   987654321

International Standard Book Number: 0-226-16552-3

CONTENTS

Part III, *Northern Illinois*

CONTENTS

PUBLISHER'S NOTE

THIS LITTLE volume was originally produced nearly thirty years ago as Occasional Publication no. 5 of the Illinois State Historical Society, under the general editorship of Jay Monaghan. It had previously been offered, we are embarrassed to say, to the University of Chicago Press and had been rejected. Printed in an edition of only a few hundred copies, mainly for distribution to the members of the society, it made very little stir in the field of architectural publishing. So far as we can discern, it was never reviewed in any public print.

Preservationism, however, and a growing regard for the domestic architecture of the nineteenth century have caught up with Drury and his gossipy chronicles of old houses and their inhabitants. Architecture buffs will find here representatives of all the prevailing styles of dwelling-house design from French colonial, through Federal, Greek revival, Gothic revival, Italianate, and Victorian eclectic to Frank Lloyd Wright—not to mention corresponding types of Illinois inhabitants.

The publishers wish that they could say with certainty which of the old houses depicted have survived the passage of time. Unhappily we cannot, although we are sure that more of these houses have resisted the depradations of developers and improvers than have this author's *Old Chicago Houses*—some thirty-four or five out of one hundred.

It is pleasant to acknowledge the help of Ellen M. Whitney, of the Illinois State Historical Library, who provided us with her own copy of the now rare original edition.

FOREWORD

FOR THE fifty-first volume of this series published by the Illinois State Historical Society we have fortunately obtained the skill of the Chicago author, John Drury, who has spent years studying and visiting old Chicago and Illinois houses—not because they are old, for John Drury is no antiquarian, but because they are, or once were, the homes of people who have helped to make Illinois history. The present volume, *Old Illinois Houses*, represents an expansion of the author's interest in the world about him—from his native city to his native state. Mr. Drury's first book, *Arclight Dusks*, a volume of Chicago-inspired poetry, was published in 1925. Three years later his *Chicago in Seven Days* appeared. In 1931 he wrote *Dining in Chicago*, and in 1933 he prepared the official Chicago guidebook for the Century of Progress Exposition of that year. While writing these volumes he served also on the staff of *The Chicago Daily News*.

As almost all of us know, half of the population of Illinois lives in Chicago. To this half belongs John Drury. It took considerable foreign and domestic travel in his earlier years, however, to make him realize that his native heath is just as good a place to write about as any other spot on earth. As a romantic-minded young man, he lived in New York's Greenwich Village, worked as a cub reporter in Los Angeles, served on merchant ships to South America and London, traveled in Canada, and cruised the Spanish Main aboard a luxury liner. In time, though, John Drury felt the call of his native Midwest and here, after returning to it, he began his writing career. In addition to his Chicago residence, he now maintains a summer home at Chesterton, Indiana.

It was just after the University of Chicago Press published his *Old Chicago Houses* in 1941 that John Drury began work on the articles which form the contents of this book. One day in the early spring of 1941, when snow floated down between gloomy Loop buildings and hissed on the cold surface of the Chicago River, he loaded into his car his wife, his dog, and his typewriter, and began the first of three circular motor tours through southern, central, and northern Illinois, totaling some 5,000 miles. His quest was historic Illinois houses. The results of his journeys appear in this book where they are reproduced from a series of weekly articles published in the *Daily News*. Having "covered" the historic-house field in his native city and native state, Mr. Drury, quite naturally, expanded his horizon again, and thus there appeared, in 1947, his *Historic Midwest Houses*. This volume involved a 10,000-mile tour of the Midwest which was made possible by a Regional Writing Fellowship awarded him by the University of Minnesota.

Readers of *Old Illinois Houses* will find this book a rather complete, though informal, history of our state. Here are described houses that represent the French period. Other chapters deal with dwellings used during the English occupation, and here, too, are residences of the American aristocrats appointed in Washington to administer the frontier government. How can anyone understand the enterprising bankers who came early to Illinois, without seeing the house of John Marshall at Shawneetown? On Rock Island stands the mansion of George Davenport, fur trader, and this expresses his affluence better than can be done in a thousand words.

Illinois as the cradle of utopian ideas in the first half of the nineteenth century appears in the homes of British idealists near English Prairie (environs of Albion) and in the residences of Joseph Smith and Brigham Young at Nauvoo. The beginning of industrial ingenuity and wealth is disclosed in the pioneer residence of John Deere, and agrarian culture at its best in the luxurious mansion of Julius Strawn. The rise of the antislavery movement is presented here vividly in the dwellings of John Hossack and Owen Lovejoy. The homes of Lincoln and Grant speak for themselves beyond "our poor power to add or detract."

For the post-Civil War period, John Drury shows us the homes of William Jennings Bryan, Dr. Greene V. Black, Jane Addams, Frances Willard, and Elbert Hubbard—all national figures claimed by Illinois a generation ago. Equally interesting are the birthplaces or homes of such renowned literary and artistic figures as Vachel Lindsay, Lorado Taft, Edgar Lee Masters, Carl Sandburg, Ernest Hemingway, and Frank Lloyd Wright. All of these were either born or reared in the Prairie State, and the houses associated with them are in this book.

In preserving the pictures and chapters in this volume, the Illinois State Historical Society wishes to express its appreciation to the management of *The Chicago Daily News* for permitting reproduction in this form. We are also indebted to Mr. Howard F. Rissler and Mr. S. A. Wetherbee, both of the Illinois State Historical Library, for ably conducting the manuscript of this work through the press.

JAY MONAGHAN.

PREFACE

IN THIS consideration of old Illinois houses, I have treated each dwelling historically as well as architecturally, but the main emphasis has been placed on the personage or event that gave it distinction. After all, more people are attracted by the home of some great man or woman, no matter how plain or lowly that home may be, than are interested in the architecturally perfect mansion of a comparatively unknown person. It was on this basis, then, that a selection (with the exception of Chicago, which I treated in a separate volume) of nearly one hundred of the Prairie State's most distinctive old houses was made, and is herewith presented.

An early and important crossroads state in the center of America's vast inland region, Illinois, I discovered at the outset of my researches, contains perhaps as many unusual historic houses as any state in New England or the Old South.

With this in mind, I began work on the material in this book. The chapters—with two exceptions—appeared originally as a series of weekly illustrated articles in *The Chicago Daily News*, starting March 7, 1941. I was then a staff member of that newspaper, having written historical articles and sketches for it since 1926. Before starting work on "Old Illinois Houses," however, I had written another series called "Old Chicago Houses." So well received were these Chicago articles that they were gathered together and published in a book of the same title by the University of Chicago Press. Having thus covered the historic houses of my native city, I felt the next logical step was to make a similar study of the domiciliar landmarks of my native state.

When I sought approval of this project by the management of *The Chicago Daily News*, it was promptly and generously given. The city editor, Mr. Lewis Hunt, and his assistant, Mr. Clem Lane, both of whom had previously fostered my "Old Chicago Houses" series, and that newspaper's then editor-in-chief, Mr. Paul Scott Mowrer, a devoted native of central Illinois, were convinced of the value of such a series as I proposed. Thus, early in the spring of 1941, in the midst of a blizzard, I began the first of my three motor tours through southern, central, and northern Illinois, journeys which in the end totaled some five thousand miles.

On visiting each historic dwelling, I took notes on both the house and its story. Then I returned to Chicago and engaged in further research on the subject, finding especially helpful the extensive historical collections in the Newberry Library. Here I was ably assisted not only by the head librarian, Dr. Stanley Pargellis, but by the two individuals in direct charge of the historical and genealogical books important to my study, Miss Elizabeth Coleman and Mr. Joseph Wolf. I also made much use of *The Chicago Daily News* library with its large collection of indexed newspaper clippings, and here, too, I was given wholehearted co-operation by its head, Mr. Thomas Sayers, whose untiring assistance I have always greatly appreciated. Others who gave me unstinted aid on historical aspects of the work were Mr. Paul M. Angle, then secretary of the Illinois State Historical Society (now director of the Chicago Historical Society), and Mr. Herbert H. Hewitt, head reference librarian of the Chicago Public Library, and his two assistants, Mrs. Roberta Sutton and Mrs. Mildred King.

In obtaining architectural information I found the most pertinent material in the Burnham Library of Architecture of the Art Institute of Chicago. Here the librarian in charge at the time, Miss Marion Rawls, was of great help, as was her then assistant, the late Mrs. Nancy Saunders. But much information on architecture, too, was offered by Mr. Earl H. Reed, of Chicago, director of the northern Illinois unit of the former Historic American Buildings Survey, and Mr. Edgar E. Lundeen, of Bloomington, director of the southern Illinois unit of the same Survey. I was also assisted on both historical and architectural matters by Mr. John T. Frederick, director at the time of the Federal Writers' Project for Illinois.

The two chapters mentioned above as not being among the original articles in *The Chicago Daily News* are those on "Keepsake Cottage" at Princeton and "Indian Terrace" at Rockford. Both of these unusual landmarks came to my attention after the newspaper series was completed. As to the question of including here the houses of living persons, such as Carl Sandburg, Frank Lloyd Wright, and Ernest Hemingway, I am sure most people will agree with me that those in this book have acquired more than passing distinction in the cultural history of Illinois.

In point of chronological order, this work should have preceded my *Historic Midwest Houses*, which was published by the University of Minnesota Press in 1947. Perhaps I should explain, also, that *Old Illinois Houses* might have remained buried in the files of *The Chicago*

Daily News had it not been for the favorable remembrance of Mr. Jay Monaghan, State Historian and secretary of the Illinois State Historical Society, and Mr. Ernest E. East of Peoria, a director of the Society. It was Mr. Monaghan who, in view of the forthcoming fiftieth anniversary of the Society (to be celebrated in 1949), suggested that my newspaper series would make a most fitting pre-anniversary volume, one that would be appreciated by both members and their friends. For this I am deeply grateful to Mr. Monaghan and the directors of the Society.

JOHN DRURY.

Part I, Southern Illinois

They came down the Ohio from the East, or crossed it from the South—families who wanted land, in better and larger tracts than they had ever known before. A majority of these homeseekers who settled southern Illinois came from Kentucky, Tennessee, and the Carolinas. And so today, among the rural villages and energetic cities of this section, may be found traces of those pioneer Southerners—here and there an old, plantation-style house with white columns supporting comfortable galleries, here and there a gracious garden bordered by ancient, hospitable magnolias, here and there a lace-like wrought-iron balcony that might have looked down on the Vieux Carré of New Orleans. Rarely, though, are found the rough-hewn logs and "shakes" that sheltered those who made the first clearings.

1. Cahokia
2. Prairie du Rocher
3. Kaskaskia
4. Shawneetown
5. Albion
6. Belleville
7. Collinsville
8. Carmi
9. Godfrey
10. Equality
11. Mulkeytown
12. Salem
13. Cairo

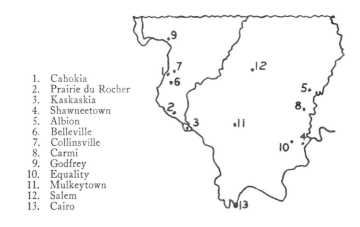

Oldest Illinois House

DURING the many years it has been revered as Illinois' most historic building, the ancient log abode now generally known as the Cahokia Courthouse was rarely, if ever, thought of as the oldest house—that is, private dwelling—in Illinois; or, in fact, as perhaps the oldest in the entire Midwest. But such it is, having been originally a dwelling house that had been built solely for this purpose. It was so used for almost half a century before being converted into a courthouse. And then, after being abandoned as a courthouse, it once more became a private home.

A family was living in this historic landmark when it was acquired in 1904 for exhibition at the St. Louis World's Fair. It was known then that various families had been occupying it since 1860. Before that it had served as a saloon and meeting hall. After the close of the St. Louis fair it was taken to Chicago and set up on the Wooded Island in Jackson Park where it remained until 1939. Now it stands on its original foundation stones at Cahokia, oldest town in Illinois. It has been completely restored, even to interior furnishings, by the state.

Of greater interest than its recent history, however, is the story of its earliest years; of the period before it became a courthouse and jail in the old Northwest Territory. The house is believed to have been built about 1737, or soon after the first white men settled in the wilderness of Mid-America. These men were French missionaries and traders from Canada who had established, a few years earlier, the Mississippi River settlements of Cahokia and Kaskaskia—outposts of the French empire in the New World.

When this log house was built, the Illinois country was part of the French province of Louisiana. The identity of the man who erected it has never been ascertained. Records show, however, that the house was later acquired by Captain Jean Baptiste Saucier, formerly an engineer in the French Colonial Army.

The house was still owned by the Saucier family when George Rogers Clark, in 1778, captured the Illinois country from the British and when, a few years later, the Northwest Territory was formed.

The first county to be organized in what later became Illinois was St. Clair County. It embraced most of northern Illinois, including the future site of Chicago. The county seat was established at Cahokia. It was in 1793 that François Saucier, son of Captain Saucier, sold the log house to the county for a courthouse and jail. Here were held the first American court sessions and the first election in the Illinois country.

2

As an indication of the great antiquity of the Saucier house, architects point to its method of construction. It is designed in the French style of pioneer log-house building—that is, with the logs set perpendicularly, as in a palisade. The later American style is characterized by horizontal logs.

Writing of this historic Illinois shrine in the June-July, 1941, *Bulletin* of the Illinois Society of Architects, a state architect, Joseph

Jean Baptiste Saucier Home, Cahokia, Built about 1737.

F. Booton, says the "structure originally had its interior walls plastered on split lath. Other refinements included casements with glass panes, shutters, beautiful wrought-iron hardware, beaded beams and ingenious roof trusses. . . . The interior had four rooms and an attic. A chimney was placed at each end and a gallery surrounded the whole."

In this very old dwelling, then, we have an example of the earliest type of shelter built by white men in the Illinois country and the Midwest. The state of Illinois, too, produced what might be termed the latest mode of shelter—the Frank Lloyd Wright home built in 1891 in Oak Park, just outside Chicago. Thus, in Illinois one may observe the whole range of American domestic architecture, from primitive log cabin to sophisticated modern home.

French Colonial Architecture

SOUTH of East St. Louis, on that fertile Mississippi River plain known as the American Bottom, lies the quiet, ancient little town of Prairie du Rocher, or "Rock Prairie." Nestling at the base of a great limestone cliff, this town is one of the oldest in Illinois, having been founded about 1722 by French colonists. These colonists had been left stranded in the Mississippi Valley when John Law's great development project, the "Mississippi Bubble," burst with a roar heard on two continents.

Among the venerable houses and cottages of Prairie du Rocher, one of the most unusual, both architecturally and historically, is a long, low, French colonial style dwelling known as the Creole House. Along with numerous other historic Illinois landmarks, this house was drawn and photographed by draftsmen of the WPA architects' project assigned to the Historic American Buildings Survey. These drawings have been placed in the Library of Congress, the Burnham Library of the Chicago Art Institute and the architectural library of the University of Illinois.

Although the draftsmen were mainly concerned with the architecture of Creole House, since it represents a type that prevailed in southern Illinois during early days, historians have found its story of wider interest than its architecture. For it is associated with several men who once attracted national attention, and in recent years it was the home of a lineal descendant of the French colonist who founded Prairie du Rocher more than two hundred years ago.

This house, however, does not date from the French colonial days of Prairie du Rocher, even though its architecture is of that period. Instead, investigation discloses that the dwelling was built about 1800, when the Illinois country was part of the newly-organized Indiana Territory and Kentuckians and others of Anglo-Saxon stock began to settle among the French in Prairie du Rocher.

Originally, Creole House was a one-family dwelling built of logs, set vertically, or in what is known as the "French-Canadian" style. In 1858, the house was enlarged by the addition of a north wing of frame construction and the whole was covered with siding. This made it, in reality, a double house. Today, it presents the appearance of a long, squat, frame abode, its low-pitched roof extending outward to form a porch the entire length of the house.

"We have never been able to determine who first built the house," said Thomas J. Conner, leading merchant of Prairie du Rocher, local historian, and descendant of an early settler. "According to one version

Historic American Buildings Survey

The Creole House, Prairie du Rocher, Built about 1800.

it was built by a Dr. Hill and another says that it was first erected by a Dr. MacDonald."

About 1830 the house was acquired by William Henry, who a few years later set up a flour mill at Prairie du Rocher. Then, in 1846, Henry's daughter, Marie Josephine, was married to Abraham H. Lee— who was subsequently to attain national prominence in an unusual way. At the time of his marriage, Lee conducted a commission house in St. Louis. Two years later, Mr. and Mrs. Lee acquired the log house in Prairie du Rocher.

"We must now drop the Lees for a moment and turn our attention to a family which rented the log house at this time," explained Mr. Conner. "This family was headed by Elias C. Hansbrough, a storekeeper of the village. In the log house a son was born to the Hansbroughs in 1848. This son was Henry Clay Hansbrough, who in his mature life became one of the political leaders of North Dakota, its first congressman, and afterward a senator from that state for eighteen years. He was sometimes called the 'father' of irrigation in the United States. For many years he was a national figure in liberal Republican politics and continued active until his death in 1933."

We are told that about 1855 or 1856 the log house came into the possession of Franklin Brickey, who was an associate of Abraham Lee in the operation of a large flour mill on the site of the original Henry mill. It was Brickey who built the north half to the log house and added siding to the entire structure. He was afterward to become president of the town board of trustees. "The most important factor in the prosperity of the village [of Prairie du Rocher] is the mill of Franklin Brickey," says a Randolph County history published in the 1880's.

It was in the year 1867 that the former owner of the log house, Abraham Lee, found himself in the national spotlight. In January of that year he was announced as the winner of a sensational lottery, nationwide in scope, which offered the imposing Crosby Opera House in Chicago as its premium. The opera house cost $600,000 to build. The lottery project was resorted to when its owner got into financial difficulties. Tickets were sold at $5.00 each. After being notified in his Prairie du Rocher home that he was the winner, Abraham Lee promptly sold the opera house back to its original owner and received $200,000 for it.

His worldly position thus enhanced, Lee built a stately mansion on a tract of land just north of Creole House and this has been a show place of Prairie du Rocher for years.

Since its enlargement, Creole House has been a double-family dwelling. After Franklin Brickey moved elsewhere, it was occupied by his son, John. The house is still owned by the Brickey estate. Surrounded by an old-fashioned cast-iron fence and shaded by several ancient maples, Creole House, with its gable roof and long, low, Southern style porch, stands as a picturesque reminder of the town's early days. Its interior walls are of plaster and the rooms are simple in design. Fireplaces, with wooden mantels, adorn the living rooms.

In the recent past, part of this house was occupied by Matthew Langlois and his family. He is a lineal descendant of Jean St. Thérèse Langlois, founder of Prairie du Rocher. Jean St. Thérèse was a nephew of Pierre Duqué Boisbriant, commandant and builder of Fort Chartres. This French stronghold has been partially restored and is now a state park and one of Illinois' most revered historic shrines.

An interesting sidelight on the United States senator who was born in Creole House is that, upon being elected to his first office, that of congressman for North Dakota, he fostered an anti-lottery bill which became a law. Although this bill was aimed specifically at the Louisiana lottery, some students wonder if it had its origin in the sensational lottery of the Crosby Opera House in Chicago. At the time of the opera house lottery, Senator Hansbrough was a shrewd, observing, idealistic young man of nineteen.

Territorial Landmark

WHAT might be considered the "Mount Vernon of Illinois," is the fine old French colonial residence in Fort Kaskaskia State Park now widely known as the Ménard house. It occupies a commanding site on a grassy bluff above the Mississippi River, some fifty miles south of East St. Louis. Surviving from early territorial days, this residence is one of the most famous in Illinois and is visited by several thousand sight-seers each year.

As with Washington's home on the Potomac, the Ménard house is now a historical museum. It is furnished with fine brown mahogany and walnut tables, chairs, chests, and other household articles which belonged to the man who made it famous.

A bronze marker and an American flag identify the house as a state-owned historic shrine. The marker explains, in part, that the house occupies a portion of Fort Kaskaskia State Park, a fifty-seven-acre tract embracing what was once Fort Kaskaskia.

This fort, which stood on a bluff above the house, was built by the French when they controlled the Mississippi Valley in the eighteenth century. The settlement of Kaskaskia was afterward to become the first capital of the state of Illinois.

In 1791, when Illinois was part of the Northwest Territory established by the newly formed American republic, there came to Kaskaskia a young Quebec-born fur trader named Pierre Ménard. He opened a store in the village, prospered, and the next year married Thérèse Godin.

Soon afterward he was appointed a major, then a lieutenant colonel of militia. When this region became part of Indiana Territory, Governor William Henry Harrison appointed Ménard a judge of the County Court at Kaskaskia. He held this position for ten years, or until Illinois became a separate territory.

After this, Ménard served as presiding officer of the Illinois territorial legislature. When the territory was admitted to statehood in 1818, with the capital established at Kaskaskia, he was elected the state's first lieutenant governor under Governor Shadrach Bond, another Kaskaskian.

In 1818 when Pierre Ménard was the general choice for the state's first lieutenant governor it was learned that he had never been formally naturalized. So the constitutional convention, in order to permit his election, altered the requisite period of citizenship, which it had placed at thirty years, making eligible for office a citizen who had resided in the state two years preceding the election.

7

At the end of his term as lieutenant governor, Ménard returned to his home at Kaskaskia, intending to spend the rest of his days in retirement with his family. But in 1828 he was again called to public duty, this time by President John Quincy Adams, who appointed him to an Indian commission headed by Lewis Cass. He was reappointed to this commission by President Andrew Jackson. These were Ménard's last public services. He died in his Kaskaskia home on June 13, 1844.

It was in 1802, just after the Illinois country became part of Indiana Territory and when Ménard was one of the best-known and most respected citizens of Kaskaskia, that he erected the house which stands today on the bluff above the Mississippi.

It was to become, according to one authoritative volume, "a place famous throughout the West for its hospitality." Several years after it was built, his wife, who had borne him four children, died. He later married Angélique Saucier, sister-in-law of Jean Pierre Chouteau, famous fur trader and Indian agent of the American Bottom.

In the years following, six more children were added to the Ménard household. But the house on the Mississippi, although broad and low in appearance, was roomy enough for them all. These children grew to maturity and lived in the house after their father's death, but one by one they moved to other parts of the country.

Meanwhile, the old French settlement of Kaskaskia below the Ménard house fell into decay as East St. Louis grew, its houses crumbled into ruin, and finally most of what was left of the original settlement was swallowed up by the Mississippi River when it formed a new channel following the flood of 1881.

After the last of the Ménard descendants left the house, it was owned and occupied for some twenty-five years by Louis Younger and his family. In 1927 the state acquired the house and the land around it. The Ménard abode was converted into a museum and gradually some of its original pieces of furniture were located and restored to it. Today, it stands as one of the oldest and most noteworthy landmarks of the American Bottom.

Pointing out that "building types brought up from New Orleans" are found in the early French settlements along the Mississippi, the WPA guidebook, *Illinois: A Descriptive and Historical Guide*, says: "Typical of these is the Pierre Ménard house near Kaskaskia. It is low and broad, of one story with the attic lighted by dormers and the roof sweeping out over a columned porch the entire length of the house." The book adds that "the design of the house recalls the minor plantation houses of Lousiana."

After leaving the walnut-trimmed reception hall, where numerous belongings of Ménard's, including his compass, Bible, spectacles, watch, flute, and flageolet are on display, the visitor is shown the drawing room, with its imported French mantel, where General Lafayette was entertained when he visited Kaskaskia in 1825. Over the mantel hangs an oil portrait of Ménard. Here, too, are Ménard's cowhide trunk and his mahogany chest, walnut bed, and numerous other personal belongings.

Similar pieces of furniture and heirlooms, including Ménard's bar-

Pierre Ménard House, Kaskaskia, Built 1802.

ber chair, books (some in French), embroidered velvet vest, two-hundred-year-old clock, wardrobe, walnut swivel-chair, cherry-wood desk, bear trap, soup ladle, and sausage grinder, are displayed in the parlor, dining room, and bedrooms. At the rear of the dwelling is the stone kitchen, with its Dutch oven, huge fireplace, and enormous water basin carved out of solid stone. Beyond the kitchen stands the stone-built slave house.

Most of the windows in the Ménard dwelling still hold their original hand-pressed panes, imported from France. On the outside of one of these panes is an inscription, done with a diamond and presumably by one of the Ménard children, which contains two names, "L. C. Ménard" and "Augustin Louis Cyprian," as well as the place-name "Ste. Genevieve, Mo.," and the date "August 24, 1842."

Illinois' Oldest Brick House

ONE of the first historic landmarks to be considered when WPA architects began work on the Historic American Buildings Survey in Illinois was the venerable Jarrot Mansion at Cahokia. There were numerous reasons for this, not the least of which is that the Jarrot Mansion is perhaps the oldest brick house in the upper Mississippi Valley.

After measuring, sketching, and photographing the mansion, the architects drew detailed plans of it under the supervision of their director, Edgar E. Lundeen, for permanent preservation in the Library of Congress and in the architectural libraries of the Chicago Art Institute and the University of Illinois. This mansion was one of several hundred historic landmarks in all parts of the state thus recorded.

When the building of this residence was begun in 1799, with workmen making all of its bricks on the spot, there was no state of Illinois. Cahokia, a thriving French town of log and frame houses, was then in the Northwest Territory, a territory established by the newly formed American republic. By the time the mansion was completed in 1806, the Illinois country was part of Indiana Territory. Later, when it became a state one of the numerous receptions to the first chief executive, Governor Shadrach Bond, was held in the Jarrot Mansion. A frequent visitor here before that time, and often afterward, was Ninian Edwards, governor of Illinois Territory, and the state's first United States senator.

What brought these public officials, as well as many other leading citizens of Illinois' territorial days, to the Jarrot Mansion was the personality, influence and status of its master, Nicholas Jarrot. In the years after the mansion was completed, Jarrot reigned in it as a kind of feudal lord of Cahokia. He is said to have owned twenty-five thousand acres of land, including the present site of East St. Louis.

A native of Vesoul, France, where he was born in 1764, Nicholas Jarrot came to America in 1790, landing at Baltimore. After visiting New Orleans, he journeyed up the Mississippi River to the French settlements in Illinois. He purchased land at Cahokia in 1793, and four years later married Julia Beauvais (his second wife), daughter of a wealthy resident of Ste. Genevieve, across the Mississippi in Missouri.

When the Jarrot Mansion was completed, it became the most admired dwelling of that region. Here, six Jarrot children were born and reared. One of them, Vital Jarrot, served in the Black Hawk War, was elected to the General Assembly, became part owner of the first railroad in Illinois, and established the first newspaper in East St. Louis.

10

In the ballroom on the second floor of the Jarrot Mansion was held the first school in Cahokia. This was in 1809 when Jarrot persuaded a lawyer from Kentucky, Samuel Davidson, to give up his practice and become a schoolmaster, at a salary of $400 a year.

Living almost next door to the Church of the Holy Family, Nicholas and Mme. Jarrot were a devout couple and always led the family procession to mass on Sundays and holy days. They were also a generous and hospitable couple, and balls, receptions, and dinners were frequent in their stately brick mansion. Here Nicholas Jarrot continued to live until his death in 1820.

During the great Mississippi River flood of 1844, Mme. Jarrot and her family went to and from their home in skiffs, tying the boats to the railing of the stairway in the central reception hall.

Although Cahokia declined rapidly with the rise of St. Louis and East St. Louis, the widowed Mme. Jarrot remained in her mansion for many years. But she left it finally and died in East St. Louis in 1875 at the age of ninety-five.

Her daughter, Mrs. James L. Brackett, occupied the historic dwelling until her own death in 1886. Afterward, the house was occupied by nuns of the near-by Church of the Holy Family, a church which grew out of the first mission founded at Cahokia in 1699.

The mansion is one of the few landmarks left in old Cahokia—which now is but a filling-station hamlet just south of East St. Louis.

Nicholas Jarrot Mansion, Cahokia, Completed 1806.

Despite its great age and the disturbances of earthquakes and floods, the house is in sound condition. On its rear wall can be seen a crack—memento of the 1811 earthquake.

It is a two-story abode of red brick, designed in the Georgian Colonial style which is evident in the white columns of the portico and in the fan-light over the paneled walnut door.

In many of the windows one can see the original hand-pressed panes, imported from France. The gabled roof is covered with modern tiles. The foundation walls, composed of rough stone blocks, are two feet thick. One portion of the dark, stone-paved basement was used as a wine cellar and storage room, and another, containing a large crude fireplace, was evidently the kitchen where Negroes did the family cooking.

In recent years a handful of children, among them dark-eyed descendants of early French settlers of Cahokia, were taught here by black-cowled nuns from the Holy Family Church—just as children were taught in the ballroom of this mansion more than a hundred years ago.

The Jarrot Mansion was showing signs of considerable wear and tear when, recently, it was purchased by Oliver Lafayette Parks of East St. Louis who, after restoring it, converted it into a residence and guest house. Parks Air College occupies a large airfield near by. Appreciating the historic value of his newly-acquired house, Mr. Parks commissioned the St. Louis architectural firm of Study, Farrar & Majers (working in collaboration with another architectural firm, Hoener & Hubbard) to restore it as nearly as possible to its original state. The result of their work is considered a fine example of early American architecture.

On the Ohio

BESIDE the levee on the Illinois side of the Ohio River, in historic old Shawneetown, there stands a small brick dwelling that has become a landmark of the state. Originally built as a private home, this ancient abode is of general interest as the place which housed Illinois' first bank. Locally it is known as the first brick house in Shawneetown and as the third brick house in the upper Mississippi Valley.

When the occupant of this house set up the state's first bank here in 1816, the town in which he lived had become an important commercial center and gateway to the Illinois territory and the West. Down the Ohio River, in flatboats, came immigrants to Illinois from Virginia and other eastern states and most of them entered the new country through Shawneetown. Here the government established a land office and here business houses flourished.

A legend is current in Shawneetown that once, in the early days, a group of Chicago businessmen rode three hundred miles on horseback to negotiate a loan from the bank in the brick house overlooking the Ohio. They described Chicago, then a village, in glowing terms. But the loan was not granted. The local bank refused it on the ground that the village of Chicago was so far from Shawneetown that it could never amount to anything.

The man who established the bank in the little, two-story brick house was John Marshall, merchant, leading citizen of pioneer Shawneetown, and scion of an old English family. About 1800 his father, Samuel, who was then living in Ireland, bought property in America—specifically in Shawneetown. But he never came to America to claim it. His three sons, however, came to this country in 1804 and settled in Shawneetown. One of these was Samuel K. Marshall, who became a lawyer, soldier, statesman, and friend of Lincoln.

It was in 1808 that John Marshall built the brick house that was to become the state's first bank. "It was a remarkable structure for its time and contrasted sharply with the log cabins and crude frame buildings of the Shawneetown of that day," writes Otis Winn for the Historic American Buildings Survey.

The house, continues Winn, "was a proper setting for the prosperous merchant and banker and his devout and gracious wife, who prevailed upon her husband to promote the building of a badly needed church for Shawneetown. Their home soon became the center of social, business and political activities. It was in this building that Marshall had his

13

Historic American Buildings Survey

John Marshall House, Shawneetown, Built 1808.

store, and in which, in 1816, he opened the first bank in Illinois. This bank was authorized by the Illinois territorial legislature at Kaskaskia, but because the territory did not back it, the bank issued its own certificates."

Winn says that after the panic of 1837 the bank could not meet the demands of its creditors and a few years later was forced to close. Since that time, the house has been occupied successively by numerous families and has been, at intervals, partly under water during Ohio River floods. Its interior is plain but roomy and has been little altered since the days of John Marshall. A second-floor porch, leading out to the high levee, was added since the great flood of 1937.

Survivor of English Prairie

IN SOUTHEASTERN Illinois, on the rich, rolling prairie between the Wabash and Little Wabash rivers, stands the small, thriving city of Albion, seat of Edwards County. More than a hundred years ago Albion was well known in America and England as the center of a semi-utopian colony of British immigrant-farmers called English Prairie. The name of English Prairie has since disappeared but one of the original buildings of the colony remains in Albion, the Gibson Harris house. It is now held in veneration as that city's oldest residence.

Although this dwelling, made of brick and located half a block west of the Courthouse Square, was constructed at the time English Prairie was in its prime, it was not built for one of the English colonists, but for an American who had come west from his birthplace on the Atlantic seaboard. This man, Francis Dickson, was one of several hundred Americans who had joined the Englishmen in setting up the colony on the Illinois prairie. After this community was established, Robert Owen and his son came from Scotland and founded a similar and more famous colony across the Wabash River at New Harmony, Indiana.

The old brick house in Albion is believed to be that city's first brick dwelling. It has the further distinction of being owned and occupied by members of the same family, that of Gibson Harris, for more than one hundred and twenty years—an unusual record for Illinois.

The man for whom the brick house was built, Francis Dickson, had conducted a general store in his home. Here he sold supplies to the English colonists, many of whom had been sailors. Among his customers were the two men who had founded the colony, Morris Birkbeck and George Flower. Both of them liberals and idealists, as well as practical farmers, these two Englishmen wrote books and pamphlets about their settlement that made it widely known in the early nineteenth century.

One of the best-known of these books was Birkbeck's *Letters from Illinois*, published the same year the colony was founded, 1818 (which was the same year Illinois was admitted to statehood). He also wrote *Notes on a Journey in America*, which described his trip from the Atlantic seaboard to Illinois. At the same time, George Flower penned many letters to English newspapers describing the colony. In later years he was to write an authoritative *History of the English Settlement in Edwards County Illinois*. William Cobbett visited English Prairie in the early years of its founding and described it in his *Journal of a Year's Residence in America*.

15

While Francis Dickson was tending his store at Albion, and English Prairie was flourishing, there lived at near-by Vincennes, Indiana, a young surveyor named Gibson Harris. A native of Litchfield County, Connecticut, where he was born in 1791, Harris had come West and secured employment making maps and plats of the country around Vincennes. While engaged in this work he helped plat Terre Haute. Soon after English Prairie was founded he crossed the Wabash and joined the other Americans who had associated themselves with the Englishmen.

Unable to secure work as a surveyor, young Harris found employment in Albion as a clerk in Francis Dickson's store. Several years later he married Elizabeth Woods, daughter of John Woods, cultured English-born hotelkeeper of Albion, whose book, *Two Years' Residence in the Settlement on the English Prairie, the Illinois Country*, was another of the published works which attracted attention to English Prairie and the great fertile lands of the newborn state of Illinois.

A few years after Gibson Harris bought the house and grocery store (1826) he erected a separate building for his store, this being located on his property just to the east of the brick house. Later, this store building was moved across the street and still stands. As with his predecessor in the store, Gibson Harris enjoyed the business and esteem of many of the colonists of English Prairie.

But there was one product Gibson Harris always refused to sell in his store, and that was liquor. An old history of Edwards County says of him: "In an early day he took strong grounds in favor of temperance, nor was it in words alone, but in action as well. It was the custom of the times to have liquor on sale in such establishments (general stores). This he would not do. Years afterward this was imputed to him as a virtue, though at the time his customers thought it a hardship."

After selling his house and store, Francis Dickson entered other fields. In his later life he lived at Louisville, Kentucky, where he was occupied as a bookkeeper. A brother of his, Dr. Henry L. Dickson, was a well-known physician in southern Illinois during the 1850's and 1860's.

Gibson Harris died in 1847 and the operation of the store was continued by his widow with the aid of three of her sons. Another son, Gibson, Jr., studied law at Springfield under Abraham Lincoln but afterward gave up law and went to Cincinnati where he became wealthy as a mattress manufacturer. It is said that he turned down an offer of a government post from President Lincoln, feeling that he was doing well enough in the mattress business.

The Harris house is a two-story, gable-roofed dwelling, its old brick walls painted a dull yellow. It is one of the few houses in Albion built

Gibson Harris House, Albion, Built about 1818.

flush against the sidewalk. Originally, the house contained only four rooms but it was enlarged and now contains nine. Most of the rooms were warmed by big fireplaces but these, with the exception of one, have have been walled up.

Among numerous Harris family heirlooms and relics of early days that were handed down from generation to generation with the house were a set of blue china dishes brought over from England by the parents of Gibson Harris' wife, a corner whatnot, an old-fashioned walnut parlor organ, a four-poster bed, and a drop-leaf table.

In the Georgian Manner

WHEN the semi-utopian colony of English Prairie was in its prime, one of its best-known residents was George French. As a tailor and clothing merchant, he had become prosperous and highly esteemed. And the house he built then, a two-story brick dwelling in the Georgian manner, still stands. It is one of the historic landmarks of the city of Albion, which was the commercial center of the pioneer settlement of English Prairie.

Although there is no proof of it, local historians are certain that George French was among the many who were induced to come to English Prairie by reading the books and writings of the colony's two founders, Morris Birkbeck and George Flower.

Originally, the early settlers of English Prairie lived in log cabins. They were mostly English tenant farmers who had acquired sufficient capital to purchase land of their own in America and who had come to English Prairie, in Illinois, because of its fertile soil and its ideal location

Historic American Buildings Survey

George French House, Albion, Built 1841.

18

between the North and South. As they thrived and prospered, they supplanted their log cabins with frame and brick dwellings.

Just when George French arrived at English Prairie has not been determined, but it is known that he built his brick house in 1841. This was at a time when brick houses were first beginning to appear in Illinois. A year after the French dwelling was built, another prominent resident of the colony, Dr. Frank B. Thompson, erected a brick house next door to the George French abode.

It is said that George French designed his own house. If so, he reproduced, in a minor way, an architectural style that was prevalent in England earlier. Here is found the elliptical arched doorway with fanlight and sidelights, as well as cornices and· stone band courses, of a typical dwelling of the Georgian era.

Situated across from the Courthouse Square at the junction of two important highways in Albion, the French house and the Thompson house (now occupied by Albion's public library) have long been noted as landmarks by passing motorists. The interior of the George French home is commodious, simple, and dignified and is enhanced by several attractive fireplaces.

For many decades this house was occupied by Elizabeth French, daughter of the original owner. She lived a quiet existence here and then, after her death some years ago at an advanced age, an interesting discovery was made in the house. It was found that Miss French had been painting pictures for many years and her oils and water colors were in practically every room of the ancient residence.

"Old Ranger" Lived Here

AMONG prominent citizens of early Belleville, old Illinois city on the bluffs east of the American Bottom, the two best known were Ninian Edwards and John Reynolds—both served as governors of Illinois. Although the home in which Ninian Edwards lived has long since disappeared, Governor Reynolds' residence survives and is one of the principal historic shrines of the southern Illinois city.

In addition to being fourth governor of the state, John Reynolds was one of the most colorful figures of pioneer Illinois, and his fame was known throughout the country and even in Europe. After his career as governor he served in Congress for many terms, headed a state junketing trip to Europe and wrote numerous books about pioneer Illinois life which are now highly prized as collectors' items. In his younger days he served in the War of 1812 and became known as "Old Ranger" because of his activities in running down Indian bands on the prairies.

From a biographical study of John Reynolds, written by Miss Maude Underwood, assistant librarian of the Belleville Public Library, we learn that he acquired his Belleville residence in 1843. The house, however, is said to have been built in 1820. Since there were clay deposits near Belleville, many of its earliest houses, including the Reynolds abode, were made of brick.

It was after the close of his congressional career in Washington that Governor Reynolds returned to Belleville and moved into the then imposing two-story brick residence. He brought with him into this house his second wife, a former Maryland girl, whom he married in Washington. She was twenty years his junior. His first wife was Catherine Dubuque, whose father was honored in the naming of Dubuque, Iowa.

"In the corner of his residential lot," writes Miss Underwood, "Reynolds erected a small one-story brick house of two or three rooms, ostensibly for a law office. But his practice of law was a secondary matter to him. His hobby was meeting and talking to people. He was content with having attained his goal and as the sunset of life approached, he began to live among his memories, which, happily for us, he recorded in printed form. Although his writings lack literary style, although there is no order or sequence of events or dates, his rambling narratives of people, places, and events fill a certain vitally important niche in Illinois history."

We are told that he purchased an old hand press and a lot of type, set them up in his law office and hired unemployed printers to produce

Governor John Reynolds House, Belleville, Built 1820.

his books, as well as pamphlets, two weekly papers, and handbills. His best-known book is *The Pioneer History of Illinois*, published in 1852. Others are *Adventures of John Kelly, Sketches of the Country on the Northern Route from Belleville, Ill., to New York*, and *The Balm of Gilead*.

Governor Reynolds died on May 8, 1865, at the age of seventy-seven. His house was subsequently occupied by a man named Netherling and afterward it was the home of Professor William Feigenbutz, leading resident of the German community of Belleville and onetime director of the locally famed Liederkranz, or singing society.

The house is still in sound condition. It contains eight rooms, in most of which the woodwork is of black walnut, plain and undistinguished. The original fireplaces remain in the main rooms. Aware of the historical significance of his dwelling, the owner, Walter D. Schmitt, correspondent of the *St. Louis Post-Dispatch* in Belleville, has placed a historical marker at the front entrance, which designates the house as the onetime home of Governor Reynolds.

It Was Unionville Then

A FEW YEARS after the four Collins brothers acquired land at a little southern Illinois settlement called Unionville—which now is a bustling city of ten thousand population known as Collinsville—they built a comfortable, two-story frame dwelling in preparation for the arrival of their parents, sisters, and a younger brother, Frederick, from Litchfield, Connecticut. This was in 1821 and that house still stands on its original site. It is now revered as a landmark not only in Collinsville but throughout the southwestern part of the state.

The Collins brothers—Anson, William, Augustus, and Michael—first came to Madison County in 1817, buying the land holdings of Unionville's first settler, John Cook. The brothers were active and energetic businessmen and soon established industries at Unionville—a sawmill, a distillery, a flour mill, and a store. They also built a small frame meetinghouse for the infant community and are said to have taken turns reading the services. The name "Collinsville" was given to the settlement when it was learned there was another village in Illinois called Unionville.

In telling of the Collins brothers, *Illinois: A Descriptive and Historical Guide* says: "The oldest brother, William, suffering a dearth of ideas for suitable sermons, wrote to the Rev. Lyman Beecher, his former pastor in Litchfield, asking for suggestions. The Rev. Mr. Beecher quickly forwarded six temperance tracts, the substance of which William passed on to his congregation.

"After one of these sermons on abstemiousness, so it is said, his wife asked: 'Doesn't it look peculiar to be preaching against strong drink on Sunday and then be making and selling whisky on Monday?' William wrestled with his conscience and the following day wrecked the distillery."

It is recorded that William's brothers agreed with him in quitting the whisky business. They afterward separated, William alone remaining in Collinsville. The other four settled in other parts of the state, and in St. Louis, established business enterprises, founded families, and did their share in helping to build up the country.

However, it may even be said of William B. Collins that he was the "father" of Collinsville. It was he who donated to Collinsville the ground for a city hall, as well as sites for a public school and for the Presbyterian Church, and for a parsonage and cemetery. He died at Collinsville in 1835. His widow and three children survived him.

22

The old Collins home is described at some length in a printed volume, *The Collins Family*, written by William H. Collins and published at Quincy, in 1897. At the time this book was printed, the house was occupied by Elizabeth A. Collins Reed and her children. Five generations of the Collins family had lived in the house, the book discloses.

"The joists were made of oak trees hewn to a straight edge on one side to receive the floor," says the book. "The weatherboards were of

William B. Collins House, Collinsville, Built 1821.

black walnut. In the kitchen was a huge brick oven about four by six feet. . . . Grape vines festooned the two-story porch in the front of the house. . . . Under the entire house was a huge cellar, and often here were stored from ten to twenty barrels of cider, and from ten to forty barrels of apples . . . Locust and hard maple trees stood in the front yard, while walnut, chestnut, apple, and cherry formed a windbreak to the west and north."

A small porch has now replaced the two-story veranda which originally spanned the front of the house.

"Living Museum"

WHAT has been termed a "living museum" is the old General John M. Robinson house in Carmi. Surrounded by ancient shade trees, this low, white, trim dwelling remains serene and secure in a city that has become an exciting oil boom town, a long-settled city around which are derricks, trailers, pipelines, and other evidences of an oil bonanza. Not many of the oil men who crowd the streets of Carmi these days know that the low, white house opposite the courthouse park is one of the oldest historic shrines of White County and the lower Wabash River country.

Now identified as the General Robinson house, so-called because of his prominence in the early history of Illinois and because his descendants have occupied the house since, it was originally built by John Craw, one of the earliest settlers of White County. Believed to have been erected in the second decade of the nineteenth century, the house was constructed of logs, but these have since been covered with clapboards. It is recorded that from 1817 to 1820 the Craw house served as a temporary courthouse—a role which it again played from 1824 to 1828. During this latter period White County's first murder trial—that of Frederick Cotner—was held in the Craw house.

After General Robinson purchased it in 1835, he added several wings to the dwelling. The new occupant was subsequently to be appointed, and later elected, to the U. S. Senate, where he represented Illinois for eleven years. Later he was appointed a justice of the Illinois Supreme Court. With his passing, the house was occupied by his widow and when she died was taken over by a daughter, Mrs. Margaret Robinson Stewart. When the writer visited the dwelling in the fall of 1942 it was occupied by Mrs. Stewart's daughter, Mary Jane Stewart, and Mrs. Fannie Hay Maffitt, descendant of a pioneer Carmi family.

What made the General Robinson house a "living museum" was its great array of furniture and other household appurtenances associated with the general and other historical characters of the state and nation. Much of this furniture was purchased in the East by General Robinson and his wife when they were living in Washington. In the house, too, were a wall clock and other relics from an early Carmi tavern operated by the general's father-in-law, James Ratcliff. These articles were in use in the tavern when Abraham Lincoln was a guest there in 1840 while campaigning for Harrison.

Another Lincoln item in the Robinson home was a small silver mug which he is said to have used when it was offered to him by Patty Webb,

John M. Robinson House, Carmi, Built before 1817.

the eight-year-old daughter of Edwin B. Webb, who was General Robinson's brother-in-law and also a friend of Lincoln's. It is said that Webb at one time was a rival of Lincoln's for the hand of Mary Todd.

Other articles in the Robinson house associated with Webb (who also was a Whig candidate for governor of Illinois as well as a cousin of Harriet Lane, adopted daughter of President Buchanan) were an old candle lantern, a two-hundred-year-old mirror, a cherry table, and an oil portrait of Webb himself. Among Robinson family heirlooms were a four-poster bed, samplers, old silver, an 1849 piano, a spinning wheel, oil portraits, early books and newspapers, and old-fashioned silhouettes.

In the south room stood a venerable rosewood secretary containing a copy of John Quincy Adams' eulogy of Lafayette, delivered in 1834. It is autographed thus: "John M. Robinson from John Quincy Adams." Here, too, were letters written by Lincoln, William Henry Harrison, and Henry Clay, as well as one of the visiting cards of the wife of President Polk.

An old-fashioned English flower garden at the rear of the house adjoins a small frame building used as an office by General Robinson when he was at home in Carmi.

The Captain's Mansion

ONE of the most colorful figures of early Illinois history, a man whose life was punctuated with numerous adventures both before and after he settled in the Prairie State, was master of the old gray limestone mansion overlooking the highway just north of Godfrey. As a pioneer financier of near-by Alton this man played an important role in the development of southern Illinois. He is best remembered, however, as the founder of Monticello College and Preparatory School for Girls, one of the state's oldest institutions of higher learning.

This man was Captain Benjamin Godfrey, whose name was bestowed on the village outside Alton where he established his young ladies' college and where he lived during the latter part of his life. In view of Captain Godfrey's earlier career, it is somewhat surprising that such a man should found a college for "females." For he had been an uneducated Cape Cod shipmaster who had sailed the seven seas and had never seen the inside of a college building before coming to Alton.

After becoming settled in his many-roomed mansion, a two-story dwelling marked by spacious Southern-style galleries, Captain Godfrey set about establishing his college—and in so doing directly benefited the cause of education throughout the Midwest. For he selected as Monticello's first principal a young Yale graduate named Theron Baldwin, who was afterward to exercise wide influence as an educator.

From a memorandum on the Godfrey mansion written by the late Herbert E. Hewitt of Peoria for the Historic American Buildings Survey, we learn that the Godfrey abode was built by one Calvin Riley between the years 1831 and 1833. Captain Godfrey took possession of it in 1834 and here he lived until his death in 1862. During this time he was twice married.

"The house is built with eighteen-inch walls of local limestone, and the structural lumber is of oak and other native trees," reads Mr. Hewitt's memorandum. "The exterior millwork is apparently the work of unskilled craftsmen, both in design and execution. Although there is an occasional profile which suggests the Greek Revival, it is as though it was designed from a hazy memory. The interiors indicate a higher quality of craftsmanship, the millwork presumably being imported from New Orleans or Massachusetts. The atmosphere of the whole indicates a Southern influence."

Before moving into this house Captain Godfrey had acquired a considerable fortune through extensive financial operations at Alton in connection with Mississippi River steamboat traffic. He and an associate were then heads of the newly chartered Alton State Bank. He had come to Alton in 1832 and a year later entered the storage and commission business in partnership with his close friend, Winthrop S. Gilman. The firm prospered and became well known up and down the river.

It was in the Godfrey, Gilman & Co. warehouse, on the Alton river-front, that Elijah Lovejoy, fighting antislavery editor, had his printing

Benjamin Godfrey Residence, Godfrey, Completed 1833.

press hidden when he was killed by a down-river proslavery mob in 1837. After leaving the banking field Captain Godfrey became a railroad promoter and built a line between Alton and Springfield. During its construction he lived in a railway coach and followed the work as it progressed. This line is now part of the Alton system.

When his railroad was completed Captain Godfrey returned to his stone mansion on the outskirts of Alton and once more devoted himself to his favorite project, Monticello Female Seminary (as it was then called). He strongly felt that girls should have equal educational opportunities with boys. In carrying out this belief he contributed $110,000 to the founding of his college. He remained a trustee of the school until his death.

Before coming to Alton Captain Godfrey had led a career filled with adventure in many parts of the world. A native of Chatham, Massachusetts, where he was born December 4, 1794, he ran away to sea when he was nine, lived in Ireland for some years, served in the United States Navy during the War of 1812, became captain of a merchantman in the Mediterranean and Caribbean trade, and finally lost his ship during a storm in the Gulf of Mexico.

One account of him says that he then "set up as a merchant at Matamoros, Mexico, near the mouth of the Rio Grande, accumulated a fortune of $200,000 and was transporting it on pack-mules to the States when he was waylaid by brigands and robbed of the whole amount. He began again in New Orleans, prospered and moved in 1832 to Alton, Ill."

Not only did Captain Godfrey engage in the banking and railroad businesses, but he was also active in the land-speculation field. At one time he is said to have owned more than ten thousand acres. When he died in 1862 he held four thousand acres in the county in which he lived —Madison. He is described as a man who was "shrewd, daring, tenacious, and life on the seas and in remote trading ports had made him somewhat high-handed."

His house is a landmark of the Alton region and is often visited by historically minded persons from all parts of the state and by students of the college he founded. It is evidently little changed, except for interior furnishings, since the days it was occupied by the enterprising Cape Cod sea captain. The wood mantels on the first floor, as well as some of the interior woodwork, show the Greek Revival style of design in vogue during the 1830's and 1840's.

For the past four decades the old Godfrey mansion has been occupied by Mr. and Mrs. William L. Waters. They appreciate the historical significance of their dwelling and have kept it, as well as the landscaped grounds around it, in first-class condition. On view in the living room of the house is a large collection of Indian relics, including axes, peace pipes, farming implements, and religious and ceremonial objects. These were collected by Mr. Waters over a period of many years.

Within walking distance of the house, in a wooded tract of three hundred acres, stand the limestone buildings of Monticello College, now gray with age and covered with ivy, and across from the campus rises the spire of the venerable Godfrey Congregational Church, a striking example of Greek Revival architecture.

The Old Slave House

SOME NATIVES of the surrounding countryside say the house is haunted. They will tell you that at certain times you can hear strange moanings and wailings from the dark attic. At other times, they say, you can make out what sounds like sad Negro spirituals.

But whether or not all this is true, the big, rangy old mansion on the grassy hilltop overlooking the Saline River Valley near Shawneetown, is of distinct historic interest, not only because of its great age and the prominence of the man who lived in it, but also because of its architecture and the events that occurred in its vicinity.

It is probably one of the best-known landmarks in the southeastern part of the state. Standing in lonely isolation, its columned verandas outlined against the sky, this dwelling is now generally known down in the Ohio River country as the "Old Slave House."

In the more than one hundred years of its existence, legends and superstitions have grown up about it like climbing vines and these tales have attracted—and continue to attract—hundreds of visitors each year. It is easily accessible to motorists, being located near the intersection of State Highways 1 and 13.

From the official guidebook of the state, we learn that the sinister legends arose from the house's association with the Ohio River slave traffic. "Under the eaves on the third floor," says the guidebook, "are tiny cells, each less than the height of a man, equipped with two narrow wooden bunks. Chain anchors are embedded in the floors of these cells, and the door frames appear to have been cross-hatched with bars. A strange contraption of timbers on this floor, according to the present residents, was a torture instrument."

It was in 1834 that work was begun on this big hilltop mansion. The man who had it built, and who afterward made it well known, was John Hart Crenshaw, whose family had settled in Gallatin County in 1811.

Upon reaching maturity, John Crenshaw entered the salt-making industry—the principal industry of Gallatin County and one that made the county famous throughout the Midwest in pioneer days. Here were located natural salt wells and here, on both banks of the Saline River, were built salt furnaces for reducing the briny water of the wells into crystals.

John Crenshaw had prospered in this business and by 1834 he was ready to build a large home for himself; one that would be suitable to his station as a leading citizen. In addition to his wife, he had five chil-

dren. As a site for his new home, he chose the top of a high hill near the
little pioneer town of Equality, once the seat of Gallatin County. He
named his place Hickory Hill. The builder of the Crenshaw mansion
was William Cavin, widely known contractor and architect in early days.

The house, it is said, required some ten years to build. Architecturally, it is, as one authority puts it, an "ungainly adaptation of the
Greek Parthenon." This places it in the Greek Revival era of American
architecture. Twelve great columns, hewn from pine trees, support first

Chicago Daily News

John Crenshaw Residence, Equality, Built 1834.

and second story verandas stretching clear across the façade of the dwelling. The third floor, containing the sinister and much-storied cells,
forms a pediment of imposing, though hardly Grecian, proportion and
design. Without trees or landscaping around it, the house looks bare
and stark as it stands there on the summit of Hickory Hill.

In a detailed article on the Old Slave House, written by Barbara
Burr Hubbs for the *Illinois Journal of Commerce*, the dark little cubicles
in the attic are described as having been used "to house the slaves who
worked the salt wells and kettles. Yes, even in the free State of Illinois."
She goes on to explain: "Employers unable to secure laborers were al-

lowed to lease slaves from their owners in slave territory. This arrangement obtained especially at the salines."

We learn further that John Crenshaw "leased numbers of Negroes in Kentucky and brought them to Equality to work at his salt wells and furnaces." After working hours, these Negroes had to be closely guarded, it was said, because if any of them escaped the lessee would be required to pay the owner the full price of the slave. The "torture instrument" referred to in the state guidebook was a whipping post in which malingerers among the slaves were given bodily punishment. It is still on exhibit in the attic, as are the stuffy, dark cubicles.

There were two whipping posts. Mrs. Hubbs tells us that they were "built of heavy timber pegged together. A man of average height could be strung up by his wrists, and his toes would barely touch the lower cross-piece. What wonder that the superstitious say that mysterious voices can be heard in that attic, sometimes moaning, sometimes singing the spirituals that comfort heavy hearts."

After explaining how free Negroes in Illinois were often kidnapped, their certificates of freedom stolen from them, and how they were then sold back into slavery across the Ohio River in Kentucky, and after referring to "dark tales" told of the Crenshaw attic, Mrs. Hubbs goes on: "Whatever their truth, we have the record of one occasion when suspicion was strong. Leading citizen John Crenshaw was indicted for kidnapping by a Gallatin County grand jury. . . . The case was tried at the spring term of court, 1842. Mr. Crenshaw was acquitted."

At that time feeling was beginning to run high between pro- and antislavery factions. Soon after Crenshaw was acquitted his salt works on the Saline River were burned to the ground. There were rumors that Negroes set the works on fire in revenge for their abducted friends. But many people insisted that the fire was accidental. The salt works were rebuilt and John Crenshaw continued as Salt King of Gallatin County.

Another story told of the Crenshaw house is that its rear wall originally contained huge double doors that provided an opening large enough to admit a carriage or small wagon. A driveway led up to this entrance. The legend is that frequently, during the night, a wagon would drive into the rear part of the house and, after the doors were carefully closed, the occupants of the wagon—slaves—were hurried up a small stairway to the third-floor attic. These doors have long since disappeared and this part of the house has been remodeled into a large, comfortable dining room.

John Crenshaw died in 1871 and his widow died ten years later. A faded monument in Hickory Hill Cemetery marks their graves.

Home of the Quadroon Girl

AMONG the many colorful stories of that hilly region of southern Illinois known as "Egypt," one of the most familiar is that of the Quadroon Girl. The house in which this girl spent most of her life still stands near Mulkeytown. The original log house was built more than a century ago, but about sixty years ago it was covered with clapboards and other improvements were made. Each midsummer, when hollyhocks bloom around this house, one hears of the Quadroon Girl once again. This touching story was finally put into print by J. G. Mulcaster, historical writer of Makanda, who gave all the details in an article in the October, 1935, issue of the *Journal* of the Illinois State Historical Society.

It was on a Carolina plantation in the early years of the nineteenth century that the story of the Quadroon Girl begins. She was then a

Simpson Studio

Basil Silkwood House, Near Mulkeytown, Built 1830's.

child. Her name was Priscilla. She and the other Negro children on the plantation enjoyed a happy existence, playing games among the cabins and around the big house. And when she grew tired of playing Priscilla found pleasure in admiring the hollyhocks which bloomed in profusion on her master's estate.

Then, when Priscilla was about nine years old, the master of the plantation became ill and died. All of the Negro children, as well as their parents, were saddened by his death. In due time the master's estate was sold at public auction. And this sale included the Negro slaves, among them Priscilla. She was in a group of older slaves who became the property of a wealthy Cherokee Indian. As the Indian returned home with his slaves, Priscilla carefully guarded something in the pocket of her apron. What she had in that pocket was a handful of hollyhock seeds from her late master's garden. The Indian finally arrived at his home in the Great Smoky Mountains of western North Carolina.

Here Priscilla lived for the next few years, and, although in a strange mountain country and among strange people, she derived pleasure from the hollyhocks which the Indian had allowed her to grow. But in 1838 the government issued an order that the Cherokee tribe of Indians must move westward to Indian Territory.

Once more the Quadroon Girl had to give up her beloved hollyhocks. Along with hundreds of other Cherokees, the Indian who owned Priscilla journeyed westward over the mountains. He was not allowed to take any other property but his slaves. Finally they arrived at Jonesboro, near the southern tip of Illinois. As it was then early winter, makeshift quarters were provided until spring.

It was here that Priscilla was bought by a new master, a white man. But this purchase was a stroke of good luck for her. For her new master, who paid one thousand dollars for her, merely bought Priscilla to free her. This man was Basil Silkwood, who had come to Illinois from Pennsylvania, acquired land in Franklin County, near Mulkeytown, built himself a log house and set up a tavern in his dwelling, which in the early days was known as the Silkwood Tavern, or Half Way House, being situated halfway between Shawneetown and East St. Louis.

Basil Silkwood hated slavery. He did all he could to prevent its spread in Illinois in those early days. He was also a childless man. So he became the foster father of sixteen orphans. When these orphans grew to maturity and were married, he gave each forty acres of land. Among his charges was the Quadroon Girl. Although he gave Priscilla her freedom, she preferred to remain in the Silkwood household where she lived to be seventy years old.

During the summer months the visitor to this old home can see the hollyhocks originally planted by the Quadroon Girl—hollyhocks which reminded the woman of her carefree childhood days in the South. These hollyhocks are not of the usual variety seen in the North. They are a dwarf type and have small, red blooms. Not far from the house is the grave of the Quadroon Girl in the Silkwood lot of Reed Cemetery.

Birthplace of the Great Commoner

THREE BLOCKS south of the business district of Salem, Illinois, stands a little, old, white-painted house that is to the town what the Abraham Lincoln home is to Springfield. The reason for this is that here was born a man who, if not so great as Lincoln, was a national figure for more than a quarter of a century, playing an important role in modern American history.

This man was William Jennings Bryan. He was born in this house March 19, 1860. Now owned by the city of Salem, the dwelling is a Bryan museum containing relics and souvenirs of the "Great Commoner."

In addition to this dwelling, Salem has other memorials to the man who was thrice candidate for President and was Secretary of State in the cabinet of President Wilson before World War I. Adjoining the little house is the Bryan-Bennett Library, dedicated by William Jennings Bryan himself in 1908. It is now housed in a new building of simple but dignified architecture.

Also at Salem, seat of Marion County, is a seventy-four acre tract of land that the city has set aside as Bryan Memorial Park. Just northwest of the town is the old Bryan place, home of the elder Bryan, where William played as a boy. This country residence still stands in its grove of ancient trees and is as much visited today as the Bryan birthplace.

The little house where Bryan came into the world was built in 1852 by William's father, Silas Lillard Bryan. This was shortly after Silas Bryan had married Maria Elizabeth Jennings, who had been a pupil of his when he was a teacher at Walnut Hill, near Salem. At the time of his marriage, Silas Bryan had but recently been admitted to practice as a lawyer. Prior to this he had served as superintendent of county schools.

A striking parallel exists between the Lincoln and Bryan families. Like the Lincolns, the Bryans originated in Virginia, came west to Kentucky, then moved north to arrive finally in Illinois in 1842.

Settled in the small, unpretentious home in Salem, a home that was outfitted with furniture made at near-by Walnut Hill, Silas Bryan became one of the best-known citizens of Marion County. He was elected to the state Senate, became a judge of the Circuit Court in 1861, and was a delegate to the State Constitutional Convention of 1870. Judge Bryan served a total of twelve years on the Circuit Court.

The Bryans lived in the Salem dwelling until William was six, then they moved to their country home outside the city. After they left the

William Jennings Bryan House, Salem, Built 1852.

house in Salem it was successively owned by a number of families until finally taken over by the city and established as a Bryan memorial.

Through the center of the house runs a small entry hall; on one side is a sitting room and on the other a parlor. The two rooms constitute the museum part of the house. A kitchen and dining room are at the rear. Two bedrooms are on the second floor. A small porch stretches across the front of the dwelling.

Among outstanding exhibits in the museum are a rifle presented to Bryan when he was commander of a regiment during the Spanish-American War, the uniform he then wore, first editions of his books, the glasses he wore while Secretary of State, a watch chain made out of Mrs. Bryan's hair, pebbles gathered by Mr. Bryan on the shore of the Sea of Galilee, a temperance loving cup, an ancient typewriter, a solid silver toothpick case he used, the flag that draped his coffin, and numerous badges and other souvenirs of the Democratic convention at Chicago in 1896 where his famous "Cross of Gold" speech made him a candidate for President.

Under the Magnolias

IN THE DAYS when great white packets steamed up and down the Mississippi and Ohio rivers, and the city of Cairo at their confluence was a leading river port, there were built many imposing mansions along the magnolia-shaded streets of the steamboat metropolis. One of the best known of these, particularly in the years after the Civil War, was the Galigher house, a spacious Victorian residence at the southeast corner of Washington Avenue and Twenty-eighth Street. Construction of this noteworthy dwelling was begun in 1869 and completed in 1872.

Because of its ornate style of architecture and for the reason that it was the scene of a gala reception for General and Mrs. Ulysses S. Grant upon their return from a world tour in 1880, this house was included in the Illinois section of the Historic American Buildings Survey. However, a note in the Survey says, "This subject is not represented by drawings, the photographic record being made to show what was considered a fine home of the period. The heavy, ornate, and uneasy style of architecture of the house is expressive of the taste of the time and its prototype is found in all parts of the country."

The man who erected this imposing brick residence was Charles A. Galigher, a leading citizen of Cairo during the Civil War era. After the house was completed, it was widely admired for its architecture and its setting. The walls, it is said, are of double brick, with a ten-inch air space between to keep out the dampness of the river region in which Cairo is located. A high, white fence enclosed the original grounds and many magnolia trees were planted.

An outstanding social center during the 1870's, the Galigher mansion reached the peak of its fame on April 16, 1880, when ex-President and Mrs. Grant were guests there for two days. This was not Grant's first visit to Cairo, for during the early part of the Civil War he established headquarters there and directed the successful campaigns against Forts Henry and Donelson. He set up his headquarters in the Halliday Hotel.

As a guest of the Galighers, General Grant occupied the southeast bedroom on the second floor. The southwest bedroom was occupied by Mrs. Grant and here she displayed to the ladies of the house many trunksful of gifts and souvenirs gathered on the world tour she and her husband had just completed.

During this visit several receptions were held in the first-floor drawing room of the house, and General Grant, between puffs on his familiar black cigar, is said to have remarked on the resemblance of the Galigher drawing room to the drawing room of the White House. At the end of their visit, the Grants journeyed northward to the house which had been presented to them by the citizens of Galena. (See page 188.)

In the years following this visit, Mr. and Mrs. Galigher continued

Historic American Buildings Survey

Charles A. Galigher House, Cairo, Completed 1872.

to welcome guests in the big mansion among the magnolias. Then, in 1914, the house was acquired by Peter T. Langan, a well-known lumber dealer of Cairo. Both he and Mrs. Langan continued the tradition of hospitality established by the Galighers. They also kept the house in good repair, appreciating the fact that it was a landmark of the city. After the death of Mr. Langan his widow sold the property to the present (1948) occupants, Colonel and Mrs. Fain W. King, who have taken up the Galigher tradition where their predecessors left off.

Part II, Central Illinois

As more and more homeseekers, with their pots and pans, their children and cattle, came into the vast upper Mississippi Valley, they spread out over the grassy prairies of central Illinois. They took root and, as their worldly fortunes increased, they built comfortable houses of wood, of stone, of brick. These houses were designed like the homes their owners had known earlier in the East and South. Many were in the Greek Revival and Roman Revival styles. Also, there were houses patterned after the Georgian and French modes. On farms and in the cities appeared mansions with spacious verandas, scrollwork trim, mansard roofs, and ornamental cupolas. These were the homes of successful farmers, merchants, lawyers, and public officials of central Illinois—men who had come to the state when they were young, come with empty pockets but heads full of dreams. One of the visitors in many of these homes was Abe Lincoln, a circuit-riding Springfield lawyer and storyteller who had less in his pockets and more in his head than any of them.

1. Carrollton	12. Peoria
2. Eldred	13. Beardstown
3. Charleston	14. Virginia
4. Hudson	15. Paris
5. Normal	16. Springfield
6. Bloomington	17. Cantrall
7. Towanda	18. Lewiston
8. Quincy	19. Petersburg
9. Jacksonville	20. Bement
10. Danville	21. Urbana
11. Nauvoo	22. Decatur

English Architecture

A FEW MILES west of Carrollton, seat of Greene County and center of a long-settled argicultural region near the lower reaches of the Illinois River, stand several interesting old houses which survive from the time when, more than a century ago, a group of English colonists settled in this region and called their community Mount Pleasant. This name has since become obscure and most of the settlement's original houses have disappeared, but what few remain give evidence of English architectural origins.

One of the best of these, not only for its architecture and setting, but also because four generations of the same family have lived in it continuously, is the old Hobson house, located just west of Carrollton on the original Hobson farm. Living in it at the time material was gathered for this book was Mrs. Lansing A. Dickson, great-granddaughter of the builder and kin to the founder of Mount Pleasant. Because of her antiquarian tastes, Mrs. Dickson had preserved such a collection of family heirlooms as is rarely seen in old houses of the state. The house was a veritable museum of pioneer furniture and other household belongings.

The story of the origin of this house goes back to 1822 when Mrs. Dickson's great-grandfather, James Hobson, and his family, together with several other families, all of Cumberland County, England, decided to set sail for America. They embarked at Liverpool in the brig *Yamacrow* and made the voyage to New York in forty-seven days. Then, by wagon and flatboat, they came to Illinois and acquired tracts of land just west of Carrollton, which had been founded only a few years earlier.

From all available evidence, it appears that James Hobson erected his brick house some time in the 1820's—which places it among the oldest brick dwellings in Illinois.

"Except for a few minor changes in the interior caused by the adding of electrical equipment, a water pressure system, plumbing, and a furnace, this house is just as my great-grandfather built it," said Mrs. Dickson. "All of the brick used in its construction was made by hand on the farm, the work being done by masons, carpenters, and glaziers after they had completed work on the Robert Black home down the road. This house still stands and is the oldest in the county. Robert Black was one of the men who came over from England with my great-grandfather."

In the various walnut-trimmed rooms of this comfortable two-story dwelling were many Hobson family heirlooms—a trundle bed, four gen-

Lyle D. Stone

James Hobson House, Near Carrollton, Built 1820's.

erations of wedding dresses, five generations of peacock fans, marble-topped walnut tables, a cupboard made by Mrs. Dickson's grandfather in which no nails were used, four-poster beds, numerous old-fashioned chests, oval-framed family portraits, crockery, ancient trunks, and pioneer traveling bags.

Throughout the house were beautiful hooked and braided rugs designed and made by Mrs. Dickson herself. Especially interesting, both historically and artistically, was the wallpaper of the parlor. Here, Mrs. Dickson designed and executed by hand a paper which contained Directoire wreaths and inside each wreath were engravings of early scenes in Greene County taken from an old county atlas, dated 1873. Over the fireplace was an engraving of her own house, taken from the same atlas.

The exterior of the abode is of mellow red brick with white stone lintels, and over portions of it climbs English ivy. The style of architecture is markedly English. An attractive doorway, with fanlight and sidelights, gives entrance to a large hallway, flanked by the drawing room and a pleasant living room. And in the flower garden under a great old tree grow narcissus bulbs which were brought from England by Mrs. Dickson's great-grandmother more than a century ago.

A Pioneer Editor's Home

A FEW years ago there appeared in the *Carrollton Patriot*, published at Carrollton, Illinois, an article which started a literary argument and which once more brought attention to a small, ancient stone house situated on the lower reaches of the Illinois River.

The controversy was over the question of whether or not Charles Dickens, on his first tour of America in 1842, visited that little stone house at the time he was stopping in St. Louis. Although the dispute has not yet been settled, the small house is still worthy of attention, for it was the home of a pioneer Illinois editor, author, and scholar whose writings were widely read in his time.

That editor was John Russell. He came to Greene County in 1828 and immediately began building his house with stone from the near-by limestone bluffs. When it was completed, he called it "Bluffdale." It was John Russell who was supposed to have been host to Charles Dickens here. The story of this visit was often told by Russell's son, Spencer G. Russell, a well-known Greene County lawyer. No mention of such a visit, however, is made by Dickens in his *American Notes*, although he did describe a side jaunt of about thirty miles from St. Louis through the Illinois prairie country.

The controversy began when the *Jersey County Democrat*, published at Jerseyville, just below Carrollton, printed an interview with the Rev. J. W. R. Smith, who announced for the first time that the famous English novelist had been a guest in the Russell home. He quoted the late Spencer Russell as his authority and said that Spencer Russell had possessed a number of letters written by Dickens to John Russell but that these had been accidentally destroyed in a fire.

"Tradition records and the story is well substantiated," read the *Jersey County Democrat* article, "that John Russell met Dickens at the landing. After mutual greetings, members of the group climbed into the family coach and were driven to the Russell homestead, three miles north of the present village of Eldred.

"Following the ride from the landing, Dickens was ushered into the Russell home and seated before the great stone fireplace in the living room. There he and Russell engaged in conversation relative to topics of mutual interest. The story of that evening was frequently related by a son of the writer, Spencer Russell. At the time of Dickens' visit, the latter was fourteen years of age."

In doubting that Dickens had visited the Russell home, the *Carroll-*

ton Patriot says: "Ninety-two years after it is supposed to have occurred it is publicly disclosed for the first time that the eminent English novelist, Charles Dickens, visited Greene County in 1842 in order to meet Professor John Russell at his home at Bluffdale. . . . In all the articles relating to John Russell that have been printed in the *Patriot* it seems a bit odd that no one ever thought to tell about the visit of Charles Dickens."

The *Carrollton Patriot* continues: "The same article [in the *Jersey County Democrat*] says he [Russell] was editor of the *Louisville* [Kentucky] *Advertiser* in 1842, which was the year Charles Dickens visited the United States." Although discounting the Dickens visit, the *Carrollton Patriot* goes on to pay high tribute to John Russell as an editor, scholar, educator, linguist, and author.

The house in which Russell lived is a plain, story-and-a-half abode with a gabled roof and a small porch at its front. Plainly visible are the stone blocks used in its construction. Here John Russell was living when he was given the degree of Doctor of Laws in 1862 by the Old University of Chicago. And here he died on January 21, 1865.

Lyle D. Stone

John Russell House, Near Eldred, Built 1828.

"Walnut Hall"

ANY SURVEY of outstanding old Illinois houses would be incomplete if it did not include the home of the late Henry T. Rainey, who for almost a quarter of a century was in the national spotlight as a congressman from Illinois and who, in his later years, served as speaker of the national House of Representatives.

The old Rainey mansion, known as "Walnut Hall," is one of the two principal sights of Carrollton. The other is a heroic-size statue of Speaker Rainey himself, which stands in a landscaped park at the northern approach to Carrollton.

"The spreading, three-story brick house with imposing columns and solid black walnut woodwork throughout," says *Illinois: A Descriptive and Historical Guide*, "marks the entrance to a 485-acre model farm. Mr. Rainey was an enthusiastic farmer; during the years he practiced law in Carrollton and later as time would permit, he took an active part in the management of the farm."

We are told that "many pieces of historic or artistic value adorn the estate. Cannon and statuary of early days are about the lawn; the house is a museum of ancient firearms, swords, engravings, rare editions of books, and early American furniture. A Seth Thomas clock, once the property of Thomas Jefferson, is one item in the collection. North of the house a campground borders an artificial lake."

An event which will be long remembered in Greene County occurred in this house in 1934. This was when President Franklin D. Roosevelt came from Washington to attend the funeral services of his late friend. The nation's Chief Executive sat in the parlor of Walnut Hall, near the coffin that bore the mortal remains of Speaker Rainey, and around him, as well as on the grounds of the estate outside, was the largest collection of nationally known personages ever seen in the county. Besides, thousands of farmers and townspeople were present that day.

It was fitting that "Henry T.," as he was affectionately known, should occupy one of the old residential landmarks of Greene County. For he was a true "native son" of the region. His grandfather, William C. Rainey, a native of South Carolina who had moved westward to Kentucky, came to Greene County in 1832. He settled on a farm near Carrollton and for forty years served as justice of the peace in the pioneer prairie community.

One of his sons, John, was reared on the farm and in his mature years became a prominent real-estate man of Carrollton. John married

44

Lyle D. Stone

Henry T. Rainey House, Carrollton, Built 1850's.

a daughter of Samuel Thomas, one of the first settlers of Greene County. They had three children and one of these was Henry T. Rainey, who was to bring honor and fame to the family. He was born at Carrollton on August 20, 1860.

After receiving a high school education in Carrollton, young Henry attended Knox College at Galesburg, and finished his studies at Amherst College. He then took up law in Chicago and, upon being admitted to practice in 1885, returned to Carrollton to begin his public career. After holding several local offices he was elected to Congress in 1902 and served in that body, except for one term, until his death in 1934. With his impressive physique and thick crop of white hair, Speaker Rainey was one of the familiar figures of Washington life during the early days of the New Deal, a regime which he fervently championed.

Although he was in Washington a major portion of his time, Congressman Rainey managed to spend a few months each year in his country home at Carrollton. Here he and Mrs. Rainey maintained their farm and looked after their herds of Holstein-Friesian cattle and their Hampshire hogs. And in the many rooms of their residence the Raineys lived among souvenirs, relics, and antiques collected abroad during their Washington years.

Only a Few Left

ALTHOUGH numerous replicas of log cabins, such as the ones at New Salem State Park and Lincoln Log Cabin State Park, are in existence, not many originals of this kind of abode survive. It is for this reason and the fact that they once played an important role in the housing development of Illinois, that they deserve study.

Perhaps the best way to discuss the log cabin would be to select an outstanding example from among the few which are still standing. One of the best preserved, and one of the oldest of its type, is in a park in Charleston, seat of Coles County and of the Eastern Illinois State College and scene of one of the Lincoln-Douglas debates. This city is also on the Lincoln National Memorial Highway, which follows the path of the Lincoln family in moving from Indiana to Illinois in 1830.

Not only is this cabin a good example of what these primitive dwellings were like, but it has historical associations with Abraham Lincoln and other leaders of early Illinois. It is said that Lincoln often visited the cabin when he was traveling the judicial circuit as a lawyer, for in that day it was not far from his stepmother's house in Coles County.

Although this cabin is one of the principal sights of Charleston, being located on landscaped grounds in Morton Park, it does not stand on its original site. It was moved to this spot in 1926 from the place where it was built more than a century ago. Now the Sally Lincoln Chapter house of the Daughters of the American Revolution, the cabin is attractively furnished with authentic pioneer household articles— spinning wheels, candle molds, walnut chests—of the log-cabin era in American history.

This dwelling was built in 1832 by James Rennels, a young Kentuckian who, like Lincoln's father, had come up to Indiana and afterward moved into Illinois. He was one of the first settlers of Coles County, taking up his residence here only a few years after John Parker and his sons established themselves in the region which bordered the Embarrass River. This area later became Hutton Township, named after John Hutton, another early settler.

The Lincoln family, including Abe, moved into this part of the county at about the time James Rennels built his cabin. Here Rennels and his wife, who was the daughter of Joel Connolly, another early Coles County settler, reared a family of five boys and four girls. In the vicinity lived Rennels' father, John Rennels, who had followed his son from Kentucky. In time the vicinity became known as Rennels Settlement.

When he built his cabin James Rennels followed the construction methods of his time; the same methods used by Thomas Lincoln and his son Abe in building their log house. As almost every schoolboy of today knows, these cabins were made by placing logs horizontally on top of each other to form the walls. Not so noticeable to school children, however, is the fact that these logs were roughly squared with an adz and dovetailed into each other at the corners. Spaces between the logs were "chinked" with clay or mortar.

As to the origin of the log cabin, which was a form of construction unknown to the Pilgrims of Massachusetts in the seventeenth century,

Ed Paul

James Rennels Cabin, Charleston, Built 1832.

historians have learned little. One authority, the late Thomas E. Tallmadge, in his *Architecture in Old Chicago*, writes: "The log house, as we know it, was probably introduced into Delaware by the Swedes not before 1720." Other authorities point out that it was an outgrowth of the French style of vertical-log house introduced into the Mississippi Valley by the first white men to visit this region, the French explorers from Canada.

And so, under the elms of the attractive little park in Charleston, the Rennels cabin survives as an interesting link in the chain of housing development in Illinois.

A Famous Stepmother Lived Here

A FEW DAYS before leaving his home in Springfield for the inaugural ceremonies in the nation's capital, President-elect Lincoln paid a farewell visit to his stepmother, Sarah Bush Lincoln, who was then living in a plain little clapboarded house in Coles County. That house still stands

Sarah Lincoln House, Near Charleston, Built 1830's.

on its original site only a few miles south of Charleston and is now a much-visited Lincoln shrine, owned and maintained by the state.

Few episodes in the life of Lincoln, according to biographers, reveal his humanness, kindness, and devotion to family more touchingly than the last meeting in this house between the tall, ungainly man and the little, white-haired woman who was his foster mother; who reared him from a boy of ten until he reached the age of twenty-one. She understood her stepson better than his own father, we are told, and this understanding was appreciated by Abe Lincoln, who remained devoted to her throughout his life. As soon as he had the means, he purchased his father's farm so that Thomas and Sarah Lincoln would have a permanent home for the rest of their days.

It was a raw day in winter when President-elect Lincoln arrived in Charleston for the meeting with his stepmother. He came in the crude

48

caboose of a freight train, the passenger train he intended to take having missed connections at Mattoon. The story is told that when the locomotive of the freight train stopped in front of the little station at Charleston for orders, Abraham Lincoln, the President-elect of the United States, got out of the caboose and walked in mud, ice, and slush, with a shawl over his shoulders, alongside the freight cars to the station. Here, friends were waiting for him with a horse and carriage.

After stopping overnight at the home of Colonel A. H. Chapman, who had married a daughter of Dennis Hanks, a cousin of Lincoln's, the President-elect and Colonel Chapman drove a buggy to the home of Sarah Lincoln at the near-by crossroads village of Farmington, now known as Campbell. Here Sarah Lincoln—or "Sally," as she was called—greeted her famous stepson and was undoubtedly the proudest mother in America at that moment.

In his monumental six-volume biography of the Civil War President, Carl Sandburg poetically describes the meeting: "Sally Bush and he put their arms around each other and listened to each other's heartbeats. They held hands and talked, they talked without holding hands. Each looked into eyes thrust back in deep sockets. She was all of a mother to him."

Sandburg continues: "He was her boy more than any born to her. He gave her a photograph of her boy, a hungry picture of him standing and wanting, wanting. He stroked her face a last time, kissed good-by, and went away."

In Ida M. Tarbell's biography of Lincoln we are told that at that meeting Sarah Lincoln expressed fear for her stepson, saying she was afraid she would never see him again. To this humble house on the prairies of Coles County had come rumors that Lincoln's life might be taken and these Sarah Lincoln had heard with motherly apprehension.

As subsequent events proved, her fears were well founded. She was living in this unpretentious house when the tragic news of the assassination of her stepson was brought to her in 1865. Here she continued to live until her own death in 1869. Not far away, in Shiloh Cemetery, lie her mortal remains alongside those of her husband, Thomas Lincoln.

A short distance from the Sarah Bush Lincoln dwelling is the full-sized reproduction of the Thomas Lincoln log cabin, outstanding exhibit of the eighty-six acre Lincoln Log Cabin State Park, established as a memorial to Lincoln's father. The park comprises the major portion of Thomas Lincoln's farm. Thomas and Sarah Lincoln lived in the log cabin until the former's death in 1851. Afterward, Sarah Lincoln moved to the clapboarded dwelling.

Birthplace of a Journalist

IN THE QUIET, elm-shaded village of Hudson, just north of Bloomington, stand two attractive old frame houses associated with two nationally known men. In one was born Melville E. Stone, co-founder, with Victor F. Lawson, of *The Chicago Daily News* and "father" of the Associated Press, and in the other lived, as a boy, Elbert Hubbard, author, editor, and master craftsman. Both houses are appropriately identified by historical markers and both, despite their great age, are in good repair and still used as dwellings.

Of the two, the abode connected with Stone has the richer historical associations. For not only was it the birthplace of the noted journalist but here lived one of the founders of Hudson and here, in later years, often came Adlai E. Stevenson, once Vice-President of the United States. This dwelling is of note, too, as the first home to be built in the Hudson Colony, which was the nucleus of the present community.

At the time the Stone family was living in "Five Oaks," the owner of the house was James T. Gildersleeve, early Illinois settler, one of the founders of Hudson and a man whose descendants played important roles in the development of McLean County. As was Melville Stone's father, he, too, was a New Yorker, a native of Hampstead, Queens County. He was born there April 10, 1803, and came to Illinois in 1836.

Seeing the future possibilities of the Illinois countryside, Gildersleeve and a small group of men joined hands to set up what was to be known as the Hudson Colony. He and his brother, Joseph D., subscribed, says an old historical work, "for four colony interests, which gave them the right to nearly seven hundred acres of land, consisting of prairie and timber land, and town lots in Hudson."

It was on one of these town lots that James Gildersleeve built his house in 1837. This was the first dwelling to be erected in the colony. Other houses followed and soon Hudson was a thriving village. Here, in "Five Oaks," James Gildersleeve spent the remainder of his days, becoming the patriarch of the village. Some ten years after the completion of his house, he rented a portion of it to the Rev. Elijah Stone and thus "Five Oaks" became the birthplace, on August 22, 1848, of a great American journalist.

But the Stone family remained here only a few years, subsequently moving to Nauvoo, Illinois. Upon the death of James Gildersleeve, the house in Hudson was occupied by his son, Charles. One of the latter's daughters married Thomas W. Stevenson of Bloomington, brother of

Melville E. Stone House, Hudson, Built 1837.

Adlai E. Stevenson, congressman from Illinois during the 1870's, Vice-President of the United States in the administration of President Cleveland, and member of the American monetary commission to Europe in 1897. In the heyday of his public career, Adlai Stevenson was often a visitor to his brother's house in Hudson. Here, too, came other prominent persons of the time.

The house and its setting are unusually attractive. Now almost hidden in the shade of the five old oaks which surround it, this dwelling is a two-story, gable-roofed, frame abode, painted white, with green shutters. Here and there are ornamental details showing the Greek Revival style of architecture of the 1830's and 1840's. Inside are numerous comfortable rooms, trimmed in walnut and enhanced by inviting stone fireplaces.

Although this house survives as a reminder of the life and works of Melville E. Stone, another memorial to him stands a few miles away at the north end of Lake Bloomington. This is the Stone-Hubbard Memorial, a stone bench near a parkway entrance which is a dual memorial to both Stone and Elbert Hubbard.

His Father Was Famous, Too

WALK a block north of the granite marker in Hudson which identifies the house where Melville E. Stone was born, and you will come to another small boulder bearing a bronze plaque with these words: "On this site for 43 years lived, labored, and loved Silas Hubbard, M. D., born May 9, 1821, died May 18, 1917, and Juliana Frances Read, his wife, born November 16, 1829, died December 28, 1924. The children of this home were: Frances Hubbard Larkin, Elbert Hubbard, Daisy Hubbard-Carlock Pollitt, Mary Hubbard Heath, Honor Hubbard Easton." (Punctuation added.)

Although the plaque pays most tribute to Dr. Hubbard, who was a beloved country doctor of the region, the name on it of greatest interest to the sight-seer is that of his son, Elbert. For this plain, gable-roofed dwelling, now painted a pale yellow, was the boyhood home of Elbert Hubbard, writer, editor, master craftsman, philosopher, and famous at the turn of the century as the Sage of East Aurora.

It was in this house that Hubbard grew up and absorbed the

Elbert Hubbard House, Hudson, Built 1850's.

52

homely, salty thoughts of the Midwest frontier that were to form the foundation of his philosophy, a philosophy that found full expression in his widely read *A Message to Garcia*. Here, too, he first learned to write—a pursuit which became his chosen profession, which found an outlet in his magazine, *The Philistine*, and in his numerous *Little Journeys* books, and which made him one of the most widely read and widely quoted authors of the early 1900's.

In this house, also, Hubbard learned how to use his own hands in the making of things, a pursuit that led to his founding of the Roycroft Shops at East Aurora, New York. The products of these shops— finely printed books, art objects, articles of hammered brass and copper, embossed and hand-tooled leather novelties, ornamental wrought-iron work, heavy furniture—were familiar objects in homes throughout the country a generation ago.

Elbert Hubbard was born on June 19, 1856, in Bloomington. When "Bert," as the boys called him, was a year old his parents moved to the near-by village of Hudson. Here they occupied the frame house which remains as a memorial to the Sage of East Aurora.

In his biography, *Elbert Hubbard: Genius of Roycroft*, David Arnold Balch writes: "The little gray house in Hudson, to which the Hubbards moved from Bloomington when Elbert was a year old, was so small Mother Hubbard despaired of lodging her growing brood in its cramped quarters. Coral-red honeysuckle and rambler roses overran the clapboards in summer, with lilacs and syringa and flowering almond blooming in profusion just outside the door. The house was situated on the outskirts of the town, and back of it in summer lay the flower-covered prairies and yellow cornfields of Illinois."

When Elbert was sixteen a visitor came to the house in Hudson. That visitor gave Elbert his first start in life. He was Justus Weller, cousin of Elbert, and was head of a soap company in Chicago. Weller gave his young kinsman a job selling soap in Hudson and Bloomington. Elbert was so successful at this that he enlarged his field. He sold Weller soap all over the Midwest. Then he went to Chicago and operated from the headquarters of the Weller firm.

This was followed by his removal to Buffalo, New York, where he became a partner in a soap firm. In a few years, however, he retired from the firm with a small fortune, went to England and met William Morris, returned to America and set up the Roycroft Shops at East Aurora, outside Buffalo, in 1895. There he began the work which brought him national and even international fame.

Home of a City Founder

AT THE ENTRANCE to the campus of Illinois State Normal University—oldest teachers' college in the state, ninth oldest in the country—there stands an attractive memorial gate bearing the inscription: "To the founder of Normal, Jesse W. Fell, friend of education, lover and planter of trees, philanthropist of mighty vision, this gate is dedicated by The Women's Improvement League and his many friends." (Punctuation added.) This legend gives some information as to Jesse Fell's status in Illinois history, but it by no means tells the whole story.

Not only was he the founder of the town of Normal, but he is of much greater interest as one of the three men who made Abraham Lincoln a candidate for President of the United States. He was also a leader in the development of central Illinois, having founded, in addition to Normal, such cities of today as Pontiac, Clinton, and Lexington, and he was also a railroad promoter, an outstanding lawyer and abolitionist, and at one time was the owner of a large part of the land on which Chicago was built.

Given a man of such character and accomplishments, it is but natural that interest in the house in which he lived should be high. Fortunately, the Fell abode still stands and is now one of the most revered historic shrines of the Bloomington-Normal section. It is located at 502 South Fell Avenue, on a bluff overlooking the tree-shaded streets of Normal and the lawns of the university campus. But this is not its original location for it was moved some years ago from the site where it was built in 1856 in the center of an eighteen-acre, wooded and landscaped estate called Fell Park.

In the years following, this house became a gathering place of many noted men of the state and nation. Best known of the visitors was Lincoln, whom Jesse Fell met when he was practicing law in the early 1830's at Vandalia, then the state capital. The two lawyers became close friends and this friendship lasted until Lincoln's death. It was Jesse Fell, together with two other Bloomington leaders, Judge David Davis and Leonard Swett, who were largely responsible for bringing about the nomination of Lincoln for President on the Republican ticket at the convention held in Chicago in 1860.

Both Judge Davis and Leonard Swett were frequent visitors to the Fell house, and here, too, often came Owen Lovejoy, abolitionist and brother of Elijah Lovejoy who was slain in the abolitionist cause. Others who shared the Fell hospitality were John and Cyrus Bryant,

54

Jesse Fell House, Normal, Built 1856.

brothers of the poet, William Cullen Bryant. John Bryant was a poet himself, as well as a close friend of Lincoln's and one of the founders of the Republican Party. The Bryant brothers were early settlers of Princeton, Illinois.

A native of Chester County, Pennsylvania, where he was born to a Quaker family in 1808, Jesse Fell developed North Bloomington and helped to establish Illinois State Normal University there, after which this section of the city was called Normal. Because of the many trees he planted there, Normal is now a town of shady avenues and park-like vistas. Mr. Fell also started a newspaper, the *Observer and McLean County Advocate*, in 1837, and this was the forerunner of the present Bloomington *Pantagraph*.

In addition to having been moved from its original site, the Fell house has undergone several other changes. When originally built it contained an ornate cupola and verandas on three sides. The cupola has since disappeared, as have the porches. Evidence of the Greek Revival style used in the design of the house is seen in the classic pilasters at the corners. Still intact is a fine walnut staircase in the central hall of the residence.

A Literary Shrine

I am fevered with the sunset,
I am fretful with the bay,
For the wander-thirst is on me
And my soul is in Cathay.

There's a schooner in the offing,
With her topsails shot with fire,
And my heart has gone aboard her
For the Islands of Desire.

I must forth again tomorrow!
With the sunset I must be
Hull down on the trail of rapture
In the wonder of the Sea.

IT WAS in an unpretentious, two-story frame house in the university town of Normal that the man who wrote the above well-known poem—and many others equally well known—was born in 1864. That house still stands and is now a memorial to Richard Hovey, whose lively lyrics, expressing the spirit of vagabondia, charmed Americans of a generation ago. On the well-kept lawn in front of the house rests a boulder with a historical marker on it explaining that Hovey was born here on May 4, 1864, and that he died in New York on February 24, 1900.

The fact that Richard Hovey was born in this dwelling is enough to distinguish it, but it holds additional interest, especially to Illinoisans, as the abode of Richard's father, Charles Edward Hovey, a pioneer Illinois teacher, first principal of the famed Illinois State Normal University at Normal and a major general in the Civil War. Richard's mother, Harriette Farnham Spofford Hovey, was also an outstanding educator of her time.

When the future poet was born in this house his father was convalescing from wounds received in the battle of Arkansas Post. General Hovey's command at this encounter, the 33d Regiment of Illinois Volunteers, consisted largely of students and teachers of the Illinois State Normal University, and because of this it became known as the "Normal Regiment," and sometimes as the "Brains Regiment."

Only three years before the outbreak of the war between the states Charles Hovey had helped to establish the teachers' college. He was then a leading educator of Illinois, and in this capacity had an important

56

Richard Hovey House, Normal, Built 1850's.

part in prevailing upon the state legislature to establish a college for the proper training of common-school teachers. With one assistant and forty-three students Hovey opened the college at Normal, two miles north of Bloomington, in October, 1857, and remained head of the institution until the outbreak of the Civil War.

Although Charles Hovey played an important role in the educational history of Illinois, he was not a native of the state. He was born in Thetford, Orange County, Vermont, on April 26, 1827. After

his graduation from Dartmouth College he came west to Illinois and settled at Peoria in 1854, where he received an appointment that year as
principal of a boys' high school. Two years later he was named superintendent of Peoria's public schools.

"An able administrator and an energetic, progressive educator,"
says the *Dictionary of American Biography*, "he soon made his influence
felt throughout the state. He placed the Peoria schools upon a firm
foundation and acquired an enviable reputation as a popular lecturer on
educational topics. In 1856 he was elected president of the Illinois State
Teachers' Association and in 1857 became a member of the first Illinois
board of education."

It was some time soon after he became principal of the college at
Normal that Hovey built his home, within walking distance of the college campus. Here were born his three sons, including Richard, and here
he and his wife welcomed and entertained some of the best-known Illinois educators of their time. Still standing on its original site, the house's
address today is 202 West Mulberry Avenue.

Soon after the close of the Civil War the Hoveys sold their Normal
house, moved to Washington, D. C., with their children, and there spent
the remainder of their days. In the capital city Charles Hovey took up
the practice of law, which he had earlier studied, and his wife engaged in
educational activities. Death came to Hovey there in 1897. His son
Richard, meanwhile, was rapidly gaining fame as a poet after completing
his studies at Dartmouth.

At Dartmouth he was the college poet and students there still sing
his "Men of Dartmouth." One literary critic, Professor Percy H. Boyn-
ton, said of Hovey's college verse: "He wrote for Dartmouth a body of
tributary verse which is as distinguished as are Holmes' Harvard poems.
And he wrote for his college fraternity songs and odes which are so distinguished as wholly to transcend the occasions for which they were prepared."

A few years after leaving college Richard Hovey met another poet,
Bliss Carman, and as a result of that meeting the two afterward col-
laborated in the series of "Vagabondia" books of verse which, as one
critic put it, "took the country by storm." Hovey also turned out many
volumes of his own poetry, and his total work in this field made him one
of the leading poets of his time.

In view of Hovey's widespread fame it was but natural for admirers of his writings properly to identify the house in which he was
born. It is now one of the sights of Normal and is often visited by persons interested in the literary shrines of Illinois.

Victorian Mansion

ALTHOUGH not so old as most of the dwellings in this book, the large brick residence at 909 North McLean Street, in Bloomington, is worthy of attention as the home of one of the best-known Illinoisans of his time. This man was Joseph Wilson Fifer, nineteenth governor of Illinois and famed throughout the nation as "Private Joe" Fifer. As the "grand old man of Illinois" for more than a quarter of a century, "Private Joe" held court in his Bloomington residence and here his public birthday parties were outstanding annual events. Many people came from other parts of the state and nation to pay tribute to Joe Fifer on these occasions.

This McLean Street house, set back on a shaded, landscaped lawn across from Franklin Park, was built in 1896. It is a typical residence of the 1890's—massive, spacious, comfortable, and marked by that distinguishing characteristic of a late Victorian mansion, a hospitable veranda extending across the entire front. The house is two and one-half stories high, is of plain architecture, and has such other appurtenances of late Victorian dwellings as semi-circular bays and dormers.

At the time Fifer built his home he and four other former governors

Joseph W. Fifer House, Bloomington, Built 1896.

59

of the state were active in what was considered one of the most spectacular gubernatorial campaigns in the history of the state. This was the battle of John R. Tanner, Republican, to replace Governor John P. Altgeld as the state's chief executive. Governor Altgeld, who was seeking re-election, had been criticized throughout the state for freeing from prison two of the men sentenced for complicity in the Haymarket Riot of 1886. Altgeld had felt that the men were unjustly convicted. Most historians now agree that he was correct in this view.

During the turmoil of the campaign, however, "Private Joe" was not among those who denounced Governor Altgeld for pardoning the men. He and Altgeld were friends. It is said he even felt that Altgeld "had just grounds" for freeing the Haymarket men. What impelled Fifer to campaign against Altgeld, the Democrat, was simply his devotion to the Republican Party.

It was in the gubernatorial campaign of 1888, when he himself was a candidate for governor, that Fifer earned the sobriquet which remained with him for the rest of his life. The other Republican candidates for the nomination for governor that year were General John C. Smith, General John C. McNulta, General John I. Reinecker, Colonel Clarke E. Carr, Major J. A. Connelly, and Captain Frank Wright. Fifer was the only one who had served as a private in the Civil War. Thus he became "Private Joe" during the campaign. And, as "Private Joe," he was afterwards victorious over his Democratic rival, who was General John M. Palmer.

Many improvements and reforms were introduced into the state by Governor Fifer during his term of office. He corrected evil voting practices, introduced the pardon law, improved school laws and obtained a compulsory education enactment, and achieved economies for the state through close supervision of contracts and commissions. He ran for re-election in 1892 but was defeated in the Cleveland landslide of that year, his victorious opponent being John P. Altgeld. "Private Joe" returned to Bloomington and once more took up the practice of law.

If Fifer had planned to live quietly in his big McLean Street house, this wish was not to be realized, for President McKinley appointed him to the Interstate Commerce Commission in 1899. He was reappointed in 1903 by President Theodore Roosevelt. Three years later he resigned, once more to practice law in Bloomington. Then in 1920 he was elected a delegate to the Illinois Constitutional Convention—when he was eighty years old. But his age was no hindrance; he was one of the most active men at the convention. "Private Joe" lived eighteen years after that and died in his home on August 6, 1938.

A Vice-President Lived Here

POINTED OUT as one of the principal sights of Bloomington is the old Adlai Stevenson residence at 901 North McLean Street. It holds this distinction because here lived one of Bloomington's most noted citizens, Adlai Ewing Stevenson, who, besides having been Vice-President of the United States under President Cleveland, served his city, state, and nation in other capacities which made him a leading figure of his time.

It was in the spring of 1887, when Adlai Stevenson was already in the national spotlight, that he acquired the McLean Street mansion,

Adlai E. Stevenson House, Bloomington, Built 1860's.

which stands across the street from the landscaped grounds of Franklin Park. At that time it was one of the noteworthy residences of the city, having been built some twenty years earlier by a Mr. Dobson, successful businessman of the Civil War era. On all sides of it were similar imposing mansions, for this was then the principal residential area of Bloomington.

61

After two terms in Congress Stevenson became President Cleveland's first assistant postmaster general, and then he was elected Vice-President on the Democratic ticket in 1892. He served until 1897 and, upon retirement from that office, was appointed to the bimetallic commission by President McKinley, an assignment which took him to England, France, Italy, and Belgium.

Once again Stevenson was to be a candidate for Vice-President. This was in 1900 when he was the running mate of William Jennings Bryan on the Democratic ticket. During this political battle the Stevenson residence in Bloomington was a center of attention. It was again in the limelight eight years later when, despite his advanced age, Stevenson was an unsuccessful candidate for governor of Illinois against Charles S. Deneen. Now well along in years, the Bloomington lawyer retired from active life. In his McLean Street residence, he spent his declining years writing a book of reminiscences, *Something of Men I Have Known.*

He died in Chicago on June 14, 1914, at the age of seventy-nine. His wife, Letitia Green Stevenson, had died six months earlier. In many ways she was as outstanding as her husband. Daughter of the Rev. Lewis W. Green, a well-known Kentucky educator, Mrs. Stevenson, as chatelaine of the Bloomington residence, made it a social and cultural center of the city. She was for four years president general of the Daughters of the American Revolution, was closely associated with the Colonial Dames, was active in the Federation of Illinois Women's Clubs, and was interested in foreign missions.

After the deaths of Adlai Stevenson and his wife, the McLean Street house had a number of occupants, finally becoming a rooming house for students of the Illinois State Normal University and Illinois Wesleyan University.

Since its construction eighty years ago, this residence has undergone numerous changes and improvements. The present veranda is a later addition. The house is a spacious, three-story abode of brick. It has twelve rooms. The dining room, library, parlor, and reception hall are of interest for their fine walnut trim. Looking upward in the reception hall, one observes a dome of stained glass which canopies the winding walnut stairway.

Home of a Supreme Court Justice

JUDGE DAVID DAVIS is said to have been the one man who, more than any other, helped to bring about the election of Abraham Lincoln to the presidency. This pioneer Illinois lawyer and justice of the United States Supreme Court erected a palatial residence in Bloomington in his later years, and this dwelling survives as one of the outstanding historical sights of the central Illinois city.

Located at 1000 East Jefferson Street, the Davis house is a typical mansion of the 1870's. Set back on a landscaped lawn and surrounded by big old shade trees, its façade is dominated by a mansard tower with dormers. Still on the tower is the original cast-iron cresting—a distinguishing mark of late Victorian mansions of the more costly variety. All rooms of the house are spacious, comfortable, and decorative and reflect an era when life was more leisurely than at present.

At the time Judge Davis built this mansion he was a nationally known figure in politics. Not only had he served for fifteen years as an associate justice of the United States Supreme Court, but he had afterward been elected to the United States Senate from Illinois. At one time

United Photo

David Davis House, Bloomington, Built 1870's.

63

during this term he was president *pro tempore* of the Senate. At an earlier date he was the National Labor Reform Party's candidate for President of the United States, but was unsuccessful in the ensuing campaign.

Anyone who reads a biography of Lincoln will frequently encounter the name of Judge David Davis. For Davis was one of Lincoln's closest friends and had been such for many years before the Springfield lawyer was thought of as presidential timber. In Illinois history Judge Davis is known as one of the "three musketeers"—the three men who groomed Lincoln for the presidency. The other two, who also were Bloomington men, were Jesse Fell and Leonard Swett. Fell afterward wrote: "To Judge Davis, more than to any other man . . . is the American people indebted for . . . the nomination . . . of Abraham Lincoln."

A man of wealth, due largely to fortunate and careful investments in land throughout Illinois and the Midwest, Judge Davis had not always been of such affluence. He was born in Cecil County, Maryland, on March 9, 1815. His father was of Welsh ancestry. Because of the loss of an inheritance young Davis was forced to work his way through college. He then studied law and came to Bloomington in 1836. In 1848 he was elected judge of the famous Eighth Judicial Circuit in Illinois, over which he presided for fourteen years (1848-1862), being twice re-elected. "Many lawyers of distinction, including Lincoln, Orville H. Browning, Douglas, Leonard Swett, S. T. Logan, and Lyman Trumbull, practiced before him," says the *Dictionary of American Biography*. "An intimate friendship with Lincoln was formed during this period. . . . Lincoln at times presided over Davis's court when the Judge was pressed with private business."

In personal appearance Judge Davis was a big, impressive man, standing some six feet tall and weighing more than three hundred pounds. When seen on the streets he and the tall, lanky Lincoln were a striking pair.

"Upon the assassination of President Abraham Lincoln," wrote Burrow Diskin Good in the McLean County issue of *Illinois Quest* magazine, "David Davis, at the request of the Lincoln family, became the administrator of the martyred president's estate. His masterful handling of the affairs of this trust made a record for efficient administration of an estate."

Judge Davis died at Bloomington on June 26, 1886.

Mansion in a Cornfield

AN OBJECT of curiosity to more than two generations of travelers on the Alton (the Gulf, Mobile & Ohio) railway between Chicago and Springfield is the unusually tall old brick mansion, vaguely Italian Renaissance in design, which towers above a cornfield near Towanda, just north of Bloomington. Now used as a farmhouse, as indicated by the outbuildings around it, this dwelling is of such striking appearance that passers-by cannot help but wonder about the man who built it.

That man was William R. Duncan, pioneer farmer and stock-raiser. Research by Annabel C. Cary, a Bloomington writer, discloses that

William R. Duncan House, Near Towanda, Built 1870's.

Duncan was a native of Kentucky who had been attracted by the rich farming and pasture lands of central Illinois. When the time came for him to erect an abode suitable to his station, he purposely set out to make it impressive. Tradition says he wanted it to be noticed by travelers to and from Chicago and Springfield; he wanted it to be a show place.

Duncan evidently attained his objective. But he was destined to enjoy this pleasure but a short while. For ill luck and tragedy came with the completion of his great house. Costing thousands of dollars to build, the house greatly reduced his personal fortune. And then he was saddened by the death of his wife. He buried her in a small family graveyard adjoining his mansion. A few years later his fifteen-year-old son, Henry, was drowned in a slough east of the mansion and he, too, was buried in the family graveyard.

"Later," writes Miss Cary, "Mr. Duncan himself, while attending a fair at Decatur, was stricken with illness, and hurrying home, became so much worse he was forced to stop at Normal, where he died [in 1876] almost within sight of his home."

Known locally as Duncan Manor, this three-story mansion is designed like an "H," with the four corners marked by towers similar to those found on Renaissance buildings. It is built entirely of brick, with stone trimmings. Between the towers at the rear of the house are comfortable "galleries" which testify to the Southern origin of the builder of the house.

As this house has twenty spacious rooms, with more in the basement, it is presumed that the care of such a large establishment was to be performed by servants. Whether or not Duncan had servants has not been determined. But it is evident that the rooms in the basement, crude and of unfinished brick, were intended as living quarters for them.

It is very likely that Duncan, having come from the South, planned to staff his abode with Negro servants. And if he did, he evidently took measures to keep them within bounds, for the basement windows are protected by stout iron bars. Another feature of the house which might be connected with the maintenance of Negro servants is a mysterious trap door in one of the second-floor bedrooms which lets down into a bare, dark room. Although numerous old Illinois houses, especially in the southern part of the state, have these trap doors, leading to secret rooms, the use of this somewhat bizarre arrangement has never been satisfactorily explained.

As with all expensive mansions of the Civil War era, Duncan Manor has lofty, spacious rooms and hallways. The central hallway is especially noteworthy for its curving staircase with a fine walnut balustrade. In the walls at the landings are niches for flowers or statuary. Other features of the interior are marble fireplaces, inside paneled shutters, copper bathtubs, and ornamental chandeliers.

Quincy Museum

IT WAS a fortunate choice when, in 1907, the Quincy Historical Society selected the old Southern-style mansion at 425 South Twelfth Street, in Quincy, for its headquarters and museum. For this is the city's most historic dwelling. It is also a landmark of the state. The man who built this house more than a hundred years ago was not only the founder of Quincy, as well as of Adams County, but he was a state senator, friend and supporter of Abraham Lincoln, one of the organizers of the Republican Party, and governor of Illinois just before the Civil War opened.

That man was John Wood. As an outstanding public figure of central Illinois during ante-bellum days, he was host in his Quincy mansion to many well-known personages of the time. And it was from this mansion that, following his term as governor, he led the "one hundred day regiment," the 137th Illinois Infantry, into action in the Civil War. At that time (1864) he was sixty-six years old.

John Wood House, Quincy, Built 1835.

Although his mansion was designed in the Southern Colonial style, which was a style that copied the Greek temple mode, Governor Wood was not a native of the South. He was born in Moravia, Cayuga County, New York, on December 20, 1798. His father, Dr. Daniel Wood, was a surgeon and captain in the Revolutionary War. He was also noted as a scholar and linguist.

When John Wood was twenty years old, he left his home in New York state, came west to Illinois, met one Willard Keyes, and the two located on farms in Pike County some thirty miles southeast of the present Quincy. A year or two later Wood visited the place where Quincy now stands, was impressed with its location, and set about establishing his home there. It is recorded that Wood built a log cabin there in 1822—which was the first house to be erected on the site of Quincy. A little later Keyes built a cabin at the same place.

Soon other settlers came. As Quincy grew, John Wood's fame and fortune increased. He served as a trustee of the village and was elected mayor for several terms. In 1850 he served his first term in the state Senate. But by this time he was living in his two-story Greek Revival mansion. It was built in 1835 when Quincy was a village of log and frame houses on the east bank of the Mississippi.

From this house John Wood saw Quincy rise as a river shipping center, gazed at the great white packets going up and down the Mississippi, and witnessed the coming of the first railroads. He was elected lieutenant governor of the state in 1856 and was serving in that office when Governor William H. Bissell died on March 18, 1860. He filled out the unexpired term of Governor Bissell and then was appointed quartermaster general of the state, a position he held throughout the Civil War.

As a historical museum, the Wood home contains not only relics and mementos of Quincy's early days but also household articles, pieces of furniture, and personal belongings of Governor Wood and his family. Here is the Governor's cabinet, made by a pioneer Quincy cabinetmaker, as well as his compass, record books, mahogany desk, decanters, and a brace of Civil War pistols. Here, too, are the sword and medicine book carried by John Wood's father in the Revolutionary War.

The interior of the house, which contains seventeen rooms, is attractively outfitted with historic pieces of furniture. From the ceiling of the drawing room hangs a chandelier of French drop crystals which once graced the salon of a palatial Mississippi River steamer. The museum is open to the public. Few houses in Illinois offer a more authentic atmosphere of ante-bellum days than this old Quincy mansion.

A Cabinet Member Lived Here

LONG FAMILIAR to residents of Quincy as the St. Joseph Home for Girls, the big red-brick mansion at Eighth and Spruce streets is of historical interest as the onetime home of Orville Hickman Browning, dean of the bar in western Illinois for almost half a century, friend and supporter of Abraham Lincoln, United States Senator from Illinois, and Secretary of the Interior in the cabinet of President Andrew Johnson.

The exterior of the house is little changed since Browning's time. It stands on a block-square plot of ground bounded by Seventh and Eighth and Spruce and Sycamore streets. No longer a girls' home, it is now St. Joseph's Hospital, an institution for the chronically ill.

Like so many successful men of his time, Orville Hickman Browning, during his life, lived in three types of dwellings. First he lived in a log cabin. Then, as his fortunes rose, he built a second and more pretentious abode. Finally, when he was at the height of his career and the possessor of wealth, he built a third house; an impressive mansion that was something of a show place in its time. This is the house which is now occupied by St. Joseph's Hospital.

It was in the second home, which stood near Seventh and Hampshire streets, and which was destroyed by fire in 1904 when it was occupied by the Conservatory of Music, that Browning entertained his friend, Lincoln. Here, too, many other notable Illinois men of the period came as guests. Some time in the 1870's, however, Browning gave up this dwelling and built for himself a more imposing house, one in which he lived until his death in 1881 at the age of seventy-five. It is said that the grounds and house cost approximately $50,000.

When Browning occupied his third home, he was one of the leading citizens of Quincy. But when he first came to the city in 1831, he was an unknown young lawyer.

Browning was born in Harrison County, Kentucky, on February 10, 1806. There he studied law and, after being admitted to the bar, came up to Illinois and settled in Quincy. At that time the city was a pioneer settlement of log houses that was destined to become a steamboat capital of the upper Mississippi.

If Orville Hickman Browning was unknown when he first came to Quincy, he did not long remain so. In 1836 he was elected state senator on the Whig ticket. That same year he was married to Eliza Caldwell. His career was now started and from then he was constantly in the public eye.

"Mr. Browning," says a biography of him in the centennial edition of the *Quincy Herald-Whig*, published in 1935, was "a member of the Illinois Assembly for two years, state senator for four years, ran for Congress against Stephen A. Douglas in 1843 and against William A. Richardson in 1852. He was appointed United States Senator in 1861, on the

Orville Hickman Browning House, Quincy, Built 1870's.

death of Douglas, and was succeeded by William A. Richardson. In 1866, Mr. Browning was appointed Secretary of the Interior by President Andrew Johnson, which position he filled until the inauguration of President Grant."

After Browning's death, the big red-brick mansion he occupied was bought by Henry F. J. Ricker. It was the heirs of Ricker who gave the old Browning mansion to charity. Subsequently, a large wing of modern construction was added to the house on its south side. Here the St. Joseph Home for Girls was established.

Candlelight and Crinoline

IN THE WESTERN residential section of Jacksonville, grove-like city of colleges in central Illinois, stands the Governor Duncan mansion. Built more than one hundred years ago, the interior of this three-story house is noteworthy for its Colonial Georgian design and furnishings. The exterior was originally Georgian, with a simple, dignified façade, but this effect was marred, according to architectural students, by the addition, in the 1890's, of a narrow, three-story porch at the front entrance.

After this dwelling was completed in 1835 and its master was serving as governor of the state, it became the scene of many brilliant dinners and receptions attended by leading figures of pioneer Illinois and of the nation. Here, at various times, were entertained Daniel Webster, Abraham Lincoln, Stephen A. Douglas, and such early Illinois political leaders as O. H. Browning, John A. McClernand, and Colonel John J. Hardin. In later years William Jennings Bryan was a guest in this house, as was Anne Rogers Minor, then president-general of the Daughters of the American Revolution.

In the light of Governor and Mrs. Duncan's earlier careers, it is easy for one to understand why famous persons of the 1830's and '40's visited their Jacksonville home. For the couple had previously lived in Washington, where they were popular and widely known. Joseph Duncan was then a congressman from Illinois. After serving in the War of 1812, General Duncan was elected to Congress in 1826 where he served until 1834.

But General Joseph Duncan had engaged in public service, other than military, before going to Washington. In 1824 he was elected to the state senate from Jackson County. While he was there, says the *Dictionary of American Biography*, "his notable service . . . was his active support of a bill for the establishment of a free public school system, which became a law in 1825." The *Dictionary* also says of him: "He had little formal schooling and this lack may have been responsible for the keen interest he later displayed in the cause of popular education."

A native of Paris, Kentucky, where he was born February 22, 1794, Joseph Duncan came to Illinois in 1818, or the same year in which the state was born. He later acquired tracts of land and eventually took up farming. Then he entered politics and remained in this field during most of his life. In 1834, following his long service in Congress, he was elected the sixth governor of Illinois. Work on the construction of his Jacksonville mansion was begun the year he became governor.

71

Joseph Duncan House, Jacksonville, Built 1835.

While in Washington General Duncan attended a dinner party in the home of Matthew St. Clair Clark, who was for many years clerk of the House of Representatives. Located directly across from the White House, the Clark home, an impressive Georgian-style dwelling, was something of a popular social center.

At the dinner party General Duncan met Mrs. Clark's sister, Elizabeth Caldwell Smith, of New York City, and several years later the two were married in the Clark home. She was a granddaughter of the Rev. James Caldwell, "soldier parson" of the Revolutionary War who was killed in that conflict.

In an article on the Duncan home written by Edith Kirby Wilson of Jacksonville, we read that "Mrs. Duncan speaks of the interior plan of the Duncan house as drawn from Mrs. Matthew St. Clair Clark's home, only made smaller, and the exterior drawn from the first plan and early home of Governor Duncan at Paris, Kentucky."

An entry in Mrs. Duncan's diary reads: "In June, 1837, we entertained Daniel Webster, his wife and niece. Mr. Duncan gave him a barbecue down in the grove—northwest of the house; roasted a steer whole. Webster made a most eloquent speech, as was his wont. He took people by storm. Cheer after cheer echoed and re-echoed through the grove."

After the death of Governor Duncan in 1844, the house was presided over by Mrs. Duncan. Arrayed in her crinolines and moving against a soft background of candlelight on walnut and silver, she reigned here as a popular hostess in the Jacksonville of ante-bellum days. It was about this time that she gave the grounds in front of her Georgian mansion to the city of Jacksonville for a park. This is now Duncan Park—a restful spot of great sycamores that form an attractive approach to the old Duncan home at the north end.

Mrs. Duncan died in 1862. Then, from 1865 to 1875, the historic house was occupied by the Illinois State Institution for the Feeble-Minded, the first such institution in Illinois. Afterward the house came into the possession of a Duncan daughter, Mrs. Julia Duncan Kirby, and here she and her husband, Judge Edward P. Kirby, lived during the 1880's and '90's. While residing here Mrs. Kirby founded the Rev. James Caldwell Chapter of the Daughters of the American Revolution, named in honor of her great-grandfather.

Following the death of Mrs. Kirby the house was occupied for many years by Judge Kirby and then, with his passing, it came into the possession of Mrs. Lucinda Gallaher Kirby. In 1920 the old mansion was sold to the Rev. James Caldwell Chapter of the D. A. R., and thus it became the first D. A. R. chapter house in Illinois.

Since being taken over by the D. A. R. chapter, the seventeen-room house has undergone minor alterations on the first floor. On the walls of the vestibule, main hall, and one of the parlors hang marble memorial tablets containing the names, in gilt lettering, of pioneer Jacksonville settlers and deceased D. A. R. members. An attractive Georgian stairway, with fine walnut balusters and a landing hung with ancient draperies, leads to the second floor, where the rooms have been left intact and outfitted with some of the original Duncan furniture and family heirlooms.

Here may be seen marble busts of Governor Duncan and his daughter, Mrs. Kirby; the Governor's big, four-poster walnut bed, his carpetbag, rocker, writing desk, and large mahogany clock. Here, also, are Mrs. Duncan's inaugural slippers, her piano, music box, ancient hide trunk studded with brass nails, and a fancy French clock enclosed in a glass bell. On the walls hang several elaborate hair wreaths in shadow-box frames, one of which is said to have been made from the varicolored locks of eighty different persons. Other articles, such as candle molds, brass andirons, and bedroom china, are in this part of the mansion.

Cradle of Modern Dentistry

ON THE SIDEWALK in front of an old-fashioned white frame house at 349 East State Street, in Jacksonville, there is embedded a brass historical marker which explains that this dwelling was the home, from 1865 to 1897, of Dr. Greene Vardiman Black, now generally known as the "father of modern dentistry." This house, however, is not the only memorial to the great American dentist. A life-size statue of him stands

Dr. Greene Vardiman Black House, Jacksonville, Built 1860's.

in Lincoln Park, Chicago. At the dental school of Northwestern University his early dental office in Jacksonville has been set up as a museum exhibit. There is also a bust of him in the University of London.

In an article on Dr. Black in the *Transactions* of the Illinois State Historical Society for 1931, we are told by the author, Bessie M. Black, that "the life history of Greene Vardiman Black is the story of a self-reliant, self-educated man of rare talents and unusual ability, who contributed much to the dignity of the dental profession and to the development of science in general." The *Dictionary of American Biography* says that "he was accorded numerous honors, including the presidency of the National Dental Association in 1901, the first International Miller Prize in 1910, and honorary degrees from five institutions."

It was after serving in the Civil War, during which he was injured

74

in the knee, that Dr. Black came to Jacksonville and set up a dentist's office overlooking the public square—the same office which has been reconstructed by Northwestern University. A year later his first wife died. She was the mother of Dr. Carl E. Black of Jacksonville, who has written of his renowned father in *From Pioneer to Scientist*. After his second marriage, in 1865, Dr. Black acquired the two-story frame house in East State Street from a furniture dealer named Branson and here the dentist lived until he moved to Chicago.

At the time Dr. Black purchased this house, according to information uncovered by Miss Janette C. Powell, a Jacksonville historian and writer, he decided to combine his office and home. Accordingly, he built a two-story east wing with two rooms on each floor. The front room on the first floor was the reception room and in the other Dr. Black set up his operating room, the dental chair being placed in a bay window on the east wall. His laboratory was on the second floor.

It was in this laboratory that Dr. Black created one of the first cord dental engines. Here, too, he carried on dental experiments which soon brought him national attention. During these years, also, he wrote the first of his articles on dentistry; articles which were to grow in number as his activities widened.

"Before Dr. Black became so deeply involved in research that he had little time for recreation," writes Miss Powell, "the Black home was something of a social center and here 'open house' was always maintained to men of distinction who came to Jacksonville. For many years a 'family hour' was observed after dinner—an hour devoted to pleasant conversation and music. Dr. Black played the cello and violin well and enjoyed singing. There were several scientific groups in the town who frequently met in his home."

When Dr. Black was appointed professor of dental pathology and bacteriology at Northwestern University dental school in 1891 he spent more of his time in Chicago than in Jacksonville. Finally, when he was named dean of the Northwestern dental school in 1897, he gave up his residence in Jacksonville and established a permanent home in Chicago. There he lived and achieved renown in science; there he died in 1915.

After the departure of Dr. Black from Jacksonville the house in East State Street was occupied by his son, Dr. Carl E. Black, who became a leading physician of Jacksonville. The younger Dr. Black lived here and maintained his office here for some twenty years. The house is now owned by MacMurray College, pioneer institution founded in 1846 and located near the old Dr. Black home.

House of Art

AN OUTSTANDING example of a venerable residence that long has functioned as an art museum is the old Strawn abode in Jacksonville. During World War II, however, this imposing late Victorian mansion was converted into a Red Cross knitting and sewing center and thus it played a part in the war effort.

The man who built this house was Julius E. Strawn, one of the wealthiest and best-known men of Morgan County, benefactor of educational and religious institutions, and son of an early settler of the county. The mansion was built in 1880 and in the years immediately after its completion was regarded as an outstanding sight of Jacksonville. It became a social gathering place of the first magnitude and here the Strawns entertained many distinguished people.

The story of the Strawn family in Morgan County goes back to 1831. In that year Julius' father, Jacob Strawn, a sturdy, energetic native of Pennsylvania, arrived in the county, acquired a tract of land, and became a cattle breeder. Morgan County had been established only six years earlier. In the course of time, Jacob Strawn bought additional tracts and soon was a leading landowner and cattle raiser of the region.

At that time Jacob Strawn and his family lived in a log house at Grass Plains, a small settlement about five miles southwest of Jacksonville. In this primitive abode Julius Strawn was born on December 2, 1835. The elder Strawn continued to buy more land as he derived increased profits from his herds of cattle, which were sold in the St. Louis market. It is said that in the years before his death in 1865 he owned as much as 18,000 acres in Morgan and Sangamon counties.

His son, Julius, when ten years old, was sent to a private school conducted by the Rev. William Eddy, who afterward became a well-known missionary. Julius Strawn later attended Illinois College and, upon his graduation in 1857, went to New York and Philadelphia as an agent for his father's cattle business. He returned to Morgan County, cultivated his father's lands, and when the Civil War broke out was appointed to the staff of Governor Richard Yates.

After the Civil War, Julius Strawn toured Europe. Being a person who had early acquired a taste for painting, music, literature, and intellectual pursuits, he visited all of the leading galleries, museums, and historic memorials of the British Isles and central Europe.

In the years after the completion of his brick mansion in Jacksonville, years in which his house was the show place of the city, Julius

Strawn reigned as one of the leading citizens of Jacksonville and Morgan County. All during this time he was a trustee of both Illinois College and the Presbyterian Academy. He contributed liberally to both of these institutions and was one of the most influential persons in that part of the state.

After his death, the Strawn mansion was occupied by his widow.

Julius E. Strawn Home, Jacksonville, Built 1880.

She had long dreamed that her home should some day become a center of art in Jacksonville. This dream was realized in 1916 when her son, Dr. David Strawn, presented the house to the Jacksonville Art Association. Without much alteration of its nineteen spacious rooms, the mansion was converted into an art museum that soon attracted wide attention.

At the time he presented the house to the Art Association, Dr. Strawn began an art library which grew with the years. Many noteworthy art exhibitions were held in this house after it was converted into a museum.

A Famous Balcony

IN THE YEARS immediately before he was elected President, Abraham Lincoln was a guest in many homes throughout the central part of Illinois. When he became a candidate for United States Senator opposing Stephen A. Douglas, it was natural that, while visiting these homes, he should be prevailed upon to speak a few words to the townspeople who usually gathered before the house where he was stopping as a guest. Generally these talks were made from a front porch or from a second-floor balcony. As a result of these brief, informal speeches, the houses where they were made—that is, those which survive—have become objects of veneration to Lincoln devotees and historic landmarks in their communities.

An outstanding house of this type in eastern Illinois, and one that is noteworthy in itself as the dwelling of a well-known pioneer of the region, is the Fithian residence at 116 Gilbert Street in Danville. A large boulder on the lawn in front of the house contains a historical marker bearing the words: "Abraham Lincoln delivered an impromptu address from the balcony of this house while a guest here in 1858. Placed by the Governor Bradford Chapter, D. A. R., 1926."

In this two-story brick house lived Dr. William Fithian, one of the first settlers of Danville and a pioneer physician in that part of Illinois. He was a close friend of Lincoln's. In fact, the "Rail Splitter" served as Dr. Fithian's attorney for a number of years, representing him in several legal cases and advising him as a counselor and mentor. The two maintained their close friendship even after Lincoln became President.

When the Civil War broke out, President Lincoln, busy as he was, did not forget his friend in Danville. He appointed Dr. Fithian provost marshal of what was then the Seventh Congressional District, a district embracing most of the east-central part of the state. Dr. Fithian served honorably and competently in this capacity. After the war, he retired to his Gilbert Street home, being then in his sixties, and there held forth as one of the leading citizens of Danville.

From available data, Dr. Fithian built his house some time in the 1830's. It is of record that he came to Danville in 1830 when the city was nothing more than a settlement of frame and log houses, with a few grist mills and general stores.

In addition to his association with Lincoln and the early history of Illinois, Dr. Fithian enjoys another distinction. He is recorded as being the first white child born in Cincinnati, Ohio. His natal day was April

Tep Wright

Dr. William Fithian House, Danville, Built 1830's.

7, 1799. When William Fithian was thirteen, he served in the "home guard" during the War of 1812. Upon reaching maturity, he set out for himself, came west to Indiana, and finally settled at Danville.

As Danville grew, Dr. Fithian's practice expanded and in time he began acquiring tracts of land in the county. He entered other fields— the mercantile business, banking, politics. He served one term as state senator and two terms as state representative. When railroads appeared, he was instrumental in getting several of the leading roads to pass through Danville and Vermilion County. The town of Fithian, west of Danville, is named after him.

Dr. Fithian died April 5, 1890. Since then his house has been changed only slightly. A new roof has been added, as well as a new and larger front porch. But the ornamental, cast-iron balcony at the south end remains as it was when Lincoln stood on it almost a hundred years ago and addressed the crowd in the yard.

For more than fifty years after Dr. Fithian's death the house was occupied by Charles Feldkamp, a leading Danville confectioner, and his family. The present occupants are Mr. and Mrs. Joseph H. Barnhart and their son-in-law and daughter, Mr. and Mrs. George E. Hoffman.

Lincoln Sipped Here

AN OLD Illinois house associated with a little-known but revealing incident in the life of Abraham Lincoln is the Hooten home in Danville. Standing at 207 Buchanan Street, just east of the business district, this dwelling is one of several historic landmarks in the eastern Illinois city connected with the career of the Civil War President. As a lawyer on the then Eighth Judicial Circuit, riding from county seat to county seat on a horse or in a wagon, Lincoln was often in Danville and here he formed a law partnership with Ward Hill Lamon, whom he is said to have trusted "more than any other man." This partnership lasted for five years and brought Lincoln to Danville at almost regular intervals.

On one of these visits, it is recorded, the Springfield lawyer was taken to the Hooten home by several friends and there occurred the incident which, according to historians, threw much light on one phase of the martyred President's character. This incident had to do with liquor, for it marked the only recorded instance in his life that Abraham Lincoln ever drank anything stronger than tea or coffee. But, according to the story, there was no overindulgence on his part. Indeed, the whole episode is regarded by historians as a light, amusing incident in the life of the Emancipator; as an incident that revealed the essential humanness of America's great national hero. Lincoln himself treated it as something of a joke.

The story of what occurred in the Hooten house on this occasion is told by one of the men who was present; one of Lincoln's closest friends. This man was Henry C. Whitney, a lawyer who also traveled the Eighth Judicial Circuit and who was much with Lincoln. His book, *Life on the Circuit with Lincoln*, published in 1892, is regarded by authorities as the most voluminous and sometimes imaginative source of information on Lincoln's years as a circuit-riding lawyer.

After pointing out that some drinking was indulged in by the lawyers of the circuit, Whitney says that Lincoln "did not drink at all." He goes on to say, however, that "once I remember several of us drove out to the residence of Reason Hooten, near Danville, where we were treated to several varieties of home-made wine. A mere sip of each affected Lincoln, and he said comically: 'Fellers, I'm getting drunk.' That was the nearest approach to inebriety I ever saw in him."

At that time the Hooten house was out in the country east of Danville. During the many years since, Danville grew and expanded until it engulfed the Hooten abode and now the dwelling stands in the midst

80

of a completely built-up residential neighborhood. Situated on a grassy knoll, with only a single old oak tree shading it, the house is conspicuous for its obvious great age, although it is maintained in good condition.

When Lincoln and his friends visited the Hooten abode, the master

Tep Wright

Reason Hooten House, Danville, Built 1850's.

of the house was one of the leading farmers of Vermilion County. Near his house he cultivated a large vineyard and wine making occupied part of his time.

One of the earliest settlers of Vermilion County, coming to the region in the early 1840's, Reason Hooten had acquired a large tract of land and established a family whose descendants helped to build the present city of Danville. The house in which he entertained Lincoln was built in the early 1850's. It is a two-story home of rusty brown brick with a low-pitched, gabled roof. An addition was built on to the south portion of the house in 1890 by Reason Hooten's son, Sylvester. The fireplaces in the original portion have been removed.

Here Lived "Uncle Joe"

AMONG numerous old houses in Danville the best known was a rambling brick residence, marked by a cupola, mansard roof, and other ornamental features of Victorian architecture, which stood at 418 North Vermilion Street. This was the home, during his entire career as a picturesque national figure, of Joseph Gurney Cannon—better known as "Uncle Joe."

It was in 1876, three years after being first elected to Congress, that Joseph Cannon built the spacious house on Vermilion Street. Here he resided, between sessions of Congress, for the remainder of his life and here he died in 1926 at the age of ninety.

Before settling down in his Danville residence, Joseph Cannon had served as state's attorney. He began the practice of law at Shelbyville Illinois, in 1858, then practiced at Tuscola, and afterward came to Danville. He was born on May 7, 1836, in New Garden, Guilford County, North Carolina, where his father, Dr. Horace Franklin Cannon, was one of the founders of Guilford College. His grandfather was a native of Ireland.

As a young lawyer in Danville, Joseph Cannon won many friends by his likable personality and undoubted abilities. In 1862 he married Mary P. Reed, a native of Canfield, Ohio. After the two-story residence on Vermilion Street was built, Mrs. Cannon became its mistress and here she proved herself a worthy partner of the man who was to become known to the American people as "Uncle Joe" Cannon.

At the time the Cannon house was completed, its owner was serving in Congress. He first ran for Congress in 1870 but was defeated. Again a candidate in 1872, he was elected and served continuously in the House until 1891, when a Democratic landslide swept the country and caused "Uncle Joe" to lose his seat.

Referring to his first term in Congress, a standard biographical reference work says of him: "His uncouth manners and racy speech earned for him at once the popular appellation of 'the Hayseed Member from Illinois,' a title subsequently replaced by that of 'Uncle Joe.' "

After his defeat in 1890, Cannon came back to his Danville residence and immediately made plans to seek the office at the next election. He was elected in 1892 and served continuously in the lower house until his retirement in 1923, with the single exception of the 1913-1915 term.

Seated in his den in the roomy Vermilion Street house, "Uncle Joe" often told stories of his early days as a lawyer in Danville. And among

82

Joseph G. Cannon House,* Danville, Built 1876.

the most interesting of these stories were those concerning Abraham Lincoln, who earlier had practiced law on the same judicial circuit where Cannon began his career. "Uncle Joe" said that he first saw Lincoln at the Republican state convention in Decatur in 1860. Cannon was then practicing at Tuscola.

It was on that occasion that "Uncle Joe" heard Lincoln utter a remark that showed the dry humor of the Civil War President. Joe Cannon and a group of his friends met the Springfield lawyer at the post office in Decatur and when one of them, addressing Lincoln, expressed surprise at seeing him at the convention, Lincoln observed: "I'm most too much of a candidate to be here, and not enough of one to stay away."

Joe Cannon was in the crowd that heard Lincoln speak at the Decatur convention. He recalls how Lincoln appeared in the audience dur-

---

* Razed since this was written.

ing the convention proceedings and was immediately identified by the hundreds of delegates. Shouts of "Mr. Lincoln, Mr. Lincoln" went up from the crowd. They wanted him to speak.

"When Abe Lincoln found it almost impossible to get to the platform because of the thick crowd," said Joe Cannon, "I saw a group of huskies pick him up on their shoulders and carry him in a recumbent position to the platform. This brought cheers from the crowd."

Joe Cannon had not yet attained his highest position, that of speaker of the House of Representatives, when he was saddened by the loss of his wife. She died in the Danville residence in 1899. From that date until his own death "Uncle Joe" remained a widower, occupying the large residence with his two daughters.

In 1901 he was named speaker and served in that position until 1911. This was the period of his greatest fame as a national figure, a period when his familiar cigar appeared in cartoons all over the country.

He was offered the nomination of Vice-President of the United States in 1908 but declined, feeling he could be more useful to his country in the House. In 1916 the House commemorated his eightieth birthday with a public testimonial.

When the time came for him to retire, "Uncle Joe," between puffs on his ever-present cigar, told friends that he was going back to Danville to spend the remainder of his days in the old residence on Vermilion Street. His daughters wanted him to build a new home out in the country, but the "Sage of Vermilion County," as the newspapers sometimes called him, preferred to remain in the dwelling associated with his fondest memories.

"His principal pleasure, after leaving Congress," says a newspaper account, "was in sitting among the souvenirs of his public service. The walls of his den, and of many another room in the large house, were crowded with cartoons that appeared during his heyday, and with pictures of famous friends. He listened much to the radio, too, and read his Bible each day until his eyes grew dim. Within a few months of his death in 1926, he personally took care of all his correspondence, sitting for several hours each day at his desk dictating to a secretary."

"The Mansion House"

"AND AGAIN, verily I say unto you, if my servant Robert D. Foster will obey my voice, let him build a house for my servant Joseph, according to the contract which he has made with him." This was a divine revelation, as written down in *Doctrine and Covenants*, received by Joseph Smith, founder of the Mormon Church. It came to him, along with other revelations, on January 19, 1841. This was just two years after Joseph Smith had established headquarters for his sect at Nauvoo, a rolling, attractive region on the Illinois side of the Mississippi River.

The quoted passage was in reference to the construction of a suitable residence for the Prophet. Soon after the revelation, the house was completed by its builder, Robert Foster. It survives in Nauvoo as one

Joseph Smith Home, Nauvoo, Built 1842.

85

of the shrines of the Mormon Church, as well as a historic landmark of Illinois. In this house lived a man who played a dramatic role in American history; who founded a religion that still flourishes and who did much to develop the Western frontier.

Almost everyone knows of Joseph Smith as the founder of the Mormon Church, but few outside the Church are aware of the fact that, while occupying his Nauvoo residence, he was a candidate for the presidency of the United States.

And he was living in this house, too, when his spectacular career was brought to a tragic end. In it he was arrested following a schism within his own church and an uprising of non-Mormon people of the surrounding countryside. Arrested with him was his brother, Hyrum, the Patriarch. The two were lodged in the near-by jail at Carthage and there they were murdered by a mob on June 27, 1844.

Describing the graves of Joseph Smith and his brother, which are located near an earlier Smith dwelling in Nauvoo, the Illinois state guidebook says: "The bodies of the Prophet and his brother were moved several times after the murder at Carthage, and were finally secretly buried in a springhouse near the homestead [Smith's first Nauvoo home]. Knowledge of their location was for years a family secret; the springhouse fell into ruin; and in 1928 the bodies were found only after considerable search."

After the murder of the Prophet, the Smith home, known as "The Mansion House," was occupied by his widow, Emma Hale Smith. She was the mother of his five children, one of whom, Joseph, became, in 1860, head of the Reorganized Church of Jesus Christ of Latter Day Saints. Later known as the "nonpolygamous Mormons," this branch of the Mormon Church set up headquarters at Independence, Missouri.

Research by architects of the Historic American Buildings Survey reveals that the house and property were deeded to the Reorganized Church of Jesus Christ of Latter Day Saints in 1918 by Fred A. Smith, grandson of the Prophet. "Intensive repairs," says the Survey report, "were undertaken immediately and the house stands today in excellent condition, with most of the original details still intact."

Of white pine construction, two stories high, The Mansion House bears evidence of the Greek Revival style of design in vogue during the 1840's. This is shown by the pilasters and cornices of the façade. Now maintained as a museum by the Reorganized Church, the house contains numerous exhibits, such as Joseph Smith's desk, foreign editions of *The Book of Mormon*, early copies of *Doctrine and Covenants*, and bound volumes of the *Times and Seasons*.

A Landmark of Mormonism

A SHORT DISTANCE from the Nauvoo house in which lived Joseph Smith, Prophet and founder of the Mormon religion, there stands another landmark held in high esteem by Mormons, and particularly by the Utah branch of the Mormon Church. This is the century-old dwelling of Brigham Young, who, after the murder of the Prophet, led the

Chicago Daily News

Brigham Young House, Nauvoo, Built 1840's.

trek of the Mormons from Illinois to Utah where he established what has been called "a unique experimental society, one of the most successful colonizing endeavors in the history of the United States."

Obviously, the Brigham Young house is not so imposing as the Joseph Smith residence. For when Young built it in the 1840's he was not yet head of the church. He was then a member of the Quorum of the Twelve Apostles, ruling body of the Mormons. Soon after his dwelling was erected, however, he became leading fiscal officer of the church and his influence was second only to that of the Prophet.

A native of Windham County, Vermont, where his birthplace was but seventy-five miles southwest of the birthplace of Joseph Smith, Brigham Young grew up in New York State, became a journeyman house painter, glazier, farmer, and handyman, and then embraced the Mormon faith in 1832.

Having been a handy man in his earlier years, Brigham Young undoubtedly supervised in close manner the building of his Nauvoo house. From studies made by architects we learn that the house was constructed of somewhat crude handmade brick and that originally it was symmetrical in design—that is, with a central two-story main portion and one-story wings on the east and west sides. The west wing has since been enlarged.

Brigham Young maintained his office in the east wing which had a direct outside entrance as well as a connection with the main part of the house. The living room in the main part still retains the original fireplace, with its wood mantel. All rooms are simple in design and finished in plain woodwork. The west wing contained a kitchen, as is evidenced by the outline of a huge fireplace and bake oven, bricked up some time in the last century. There is also a brick fireplace in the basement, still usable though rarely used. At the rear of the house, and still in use, are the original well and cistern.

In the years after 1846, when Brigham Young departed from his Nauvoo house to lead the Mormons to Utah, the dwelling remained in private hands. It has not been determined whether any of the Icarians, a group of French Communists who took over Nauvoo some years after the Mormons left, ever occupied the Young abode.

In a French Communist Utopia

WHEN the Mormons left Illinois in 1847 for their great exodus to Utah they completely abandoned their once-populous city of Nauvoo on the Mississippi River. Cobwebs appeared over doorways and weeds sprang up in streets. Once the largest city in the state, with a population of more than twelve thousand, Nauvoo became a true "ghost town." But this desolate condition did not last for long. In a few years it was taken over by a large band of French Communists called the Icarians, and here they attempted to set up a utopian community.

All that survive today of the Icarian colony are two frame apartment houses and a stone school. The apartment houses stand in weather-beaten contrast to the older and sounder-built brick houses and buildings of the Mormons. Here and there through the town, however, are other evidences of the Icarian occupation—sturdy old limestone wine cellars built into the sides of gullies and depressions. Although the French Icarians remained at Nauvoo for only a decade or so, they established a wine-making industry which survived them and is today one of the two principal activities of Nauvoo, the other being cheese making.

Built sometime in the early 1850's, the Icarian communal houses are of interest both for their historical associations and as primitive forerunners of the modern apartment house. They are plain frame struc-

Frederic J. Dornseif

Icarian Apartment House, Nauvoo, Built 1850's.

89

tures, two stories high and gable-roofed. In the many rooms of these houses lived the Icarian families—married couples were allotted one room and single men were housed two in a room. Children over seven years of age were reared in the colony's school and allowed to visit their parents only on Sundays.

"The Icarians," says the *Nauvoo Guide*, written by the Illinois Writers Project, "bought twelve acres of land and built several tenements and a large assembly hall which contained a communal kitchen, refectory, women's workshop and sleeping quarters." The two surviving apartment houses stand at the northwest corner of Mulholland and Twelfth streets on the "Hill" in Nauvoo. This is the newer section of the town, the older section, where most of the Mormons built their houses, being called the "Flat." The Icarian communal houses, however, stand on part of the site of the great temple erected by the Mormons in the early 1840's, which had been destroyed by fire and storm. Near the apartment houses stands the old Icarian school, which was made of stone from the ruined Mormon temple. It is now conducted as a school by the Catholic church in Nauvoo.

This Icarian colony, one of the earliest of several attempts to set up utopias in Illinois by various European groups, was founded by Étienne Cabet, a leading French jurist who had been influenced by the teachings of Robert Owen, who also was to found a utopia in America—at New Harmony, Indiana.

"Cabet, a cooper's son, had early identified himself with the proletariat," says the *Nauvoo Guide*. "Convinced that an economic system based on the tenet 'From each according to his ability and to each according to his need' would operate to the advantage of all, he had expressed his beliefs in *True Christianity* and *Voyage to Icaria*, volumes that won a considerable little band to his form of Communism. Cabet felt that Communism should be patterned on the moral teachings of Christ, rather than on a rigid mechanistic framework."

Cabet continued to be re-elected president of the colony each year until 1856, when dissension broke out among his followers. He was defeated for re-election that year and, after making an unsuccessful attempt to regain his lost position of leadership, retired with some two hundred followers to St. Louis. He died a short time after his arrival there and was buried in the presence of only a few of his adherents. With the outbreak of dissension among the Icarians and the withdrawal of Cabet, the colony did not last much longer.

On Lake Peoria

IN THE BUSY downtown district of Peoria, not far from the big Municipal River and Rail Terminal, stands an attractive old red brick dwelling with white trim that has become one of the city's principal residential landmarks. Located on a wide thoroughfare, its quaint architecture in striking contrast to the modern buildings around it, this house dates from the years when Peoria was a prosperous river port, when the *Prairie Belle*, the *Garden City*, and other great white packets of the Five Day Line churned the waters of Lake Peoria as they got under way for St. Louis.

It was that same river traffic which helped establish the fortune of the man who built the red brick house. This man was John Reynolds, who had settled at Peoria when it was incorporated as a town in 1835. After engaging in the river shipping trade, Reynolds set up one of the first pork-packing plants in that city and later founded a beef-packing house. His products were sent down the Illinois River to the Mississippi and eventually found their way to leading Eastern and Southern markets.

John Reynolds was one of three men, all from Pennsylvania, who, lured by the call of the frontier, rode horseback to the West in the early 1830's. He and his companions—Abram S. McKinney and Hugh Williamson—arrived at the little log village of Chicago, were not impressed by its swampy location, and went down the Illinois River to Peoria. Because of its position on the river Peoria would become a great center of trade, the three men felt. They went back to Pennsylvania to get their families.

The first to return was John Reynolds. He and his wife and children came west in a crude prairie schooner. The family furniture and other household goods were shipped by boat on the Ohio River to the Mississippi and then up the Illinois River. At first the Reynolds family lived in a house which stood in the middle of the 100 block on South Adams Street. At that time Adams was a residential street. Later, as the city grew, John Reynolds decided to seek a new location for a spacious home he planned to build.

He found what he wanted on Jefferson Street. Here, in 1847, he erected the two-story brick house which still stands. Its present address is 305 North Jefferson Street. Designed by an early Peoria architect named Ulrichson, the house, architecturally, was a composite of the handsome red brick residences that John Reynolds had admired in

91

John Reynolds House, Peoria, Built 1847.

Carlisle, Chambersburg, Shippensburg, and other towns of his native Pennsylvania.

A description of the setting in which this house originally stood is contained in a family memoir written by Mrs. William Arnett of Philadelphia, granddaughter of John Reynolds. "The garden which Mr. and Mrs. Reynolds planted," writes Mrs. Arnett, "extended all the way from the house to the corner of Jackson Street. About half of this was bounded in front by an ornamental cast-iron fence, inside of which was a thick privet hedge. A path ran along this, bordered on each side by flower beds, with clove pinks growing on both sides of the path."

We are told that "the barn housed a cow and a horse. . . . Near the barn was the smokehouse, where hams and tongues were cured. In the old kitchen, with its big range, apple butter was made in the fall in a huge iron kettle, and mincemeat was made and stored in jars. Two maids were always employed and kept busy cooking, serving, and cleaning.... The children 'doubled up' in those days and occasionally trundle beds were used."

Here, in the days before the Civil War, lived John Reynolds and his wife and four children, with numerous relatives from the East paying them long visits. The master of the house was a "ruling elder" of the First Presbyterian Church and was strongly opposed to slavery. One of the sons—William—founded Calvary Church in Peoria. After the death of John Reynolds the house was occupied by his son-in-law and daughter, Dr. and Mrs. John Herschel Morron. Dr. Morron was a minister of the First Presbyterian Church.

Dr. Morron was succeeded as owner and occupant of the house by his daughter Miss Jean Morron. As chatelaine of the old Reynolds house, Miss Morron kept it and the adjoining garden in excellent condition, managing to retain much of the atmosphere of charm that prevailed here a century ago.

She was able to do this because ownership of the house has always been retained in the Reynolds family. As a result the dwelling is a veritable "period" museum. Here, tastefully arranged, the visitor may see elegant mahogany and rosewood tables, chairs and chests, as well as fine old glassware and bric-a-brac, which were brought to Illinois on an Ohio River flatboat more than a hundred years ago. In the great kitchen, a big iron range, set in red brick, is flanked by gleaming copper and brass utensils from the old days.

The New Orleans Influence

AN OBJECT that always arouses the interest and curiosity of visitors attending the annual fish fry at Beardstown, on the Illinois River, is a decorous, white-painted old house at the southeast corner of the courthouse square; a house noticeable for the fanciful iron grillwork decorating its porches. So ornamental is this white-painted fretwork that onlookers often compare it to the laciness of a valentine.

To those who have visited New Orleans, however, this sight is a familiar one. For it is a good example of the type of decoration to be found on the balconies of houses in the old French Quarter of the delta metropolis. Since architects regard it as a noteworthy demonstration of the New Orleans influence in Illinois architecture, it was included in the Historic American Buildings Survey along with somewhat similar dwellings at Galena and other Illinois towns near the Mississippi River.

A grape design was used on the porches of the Beardstown house— grape clusters and leaves interwoven with curling branches. It is of

Christopher C. Sturtevant House, Beardstown, Built 1852.

cast iron, instead of wrought metal, and the story is told that the molds used for the casting were afterward destroyed so that there would be no repetition of this design.

In obtaining the history of this landmark, Earl H. Reed, district officer of the Historic American Buildings Survey, found that the grill-work porches were not part of the original dwelling. He learned that the ornamental trim was added to the house soon after its purchase in 1865 by a Mississippi skipper, Captain Charles S. Ebaugh. In adding the fretwork trim to his porches, Captain Ebaugh desired to produce work similar to what he had seen in the Vieux Carré of New Orleans.

Although it was Captain Ebaugh who gave this house its distinctive appearance, the dwelling is named on the drawings of the Survey after the man who had it built. This man was Christopher C. Sturtevant, an early settler of Beardstown. He erected the house in 1852, designing it in the Greek Revival mode of the time. This style is noticeable in the cornices and pilasters of the two-story frame dwelling, as well as in the interior trim of the ten rooms.

After living in this house for about ten years, Captain Ebaugh sold it to John H. Harris, pioneer land agent of the Illinois River country, early Beardstown businessman, and one of the organizers and president of the First National Bank of Beardstown. Here Harris and his family lived and entertained, and here the master of the house died at an advanced age in 1911. His widow survived him by six years. The house then came into the possession of one of the Harris daughters, Mrs. Robert Burr Glenn.

During the disastrous flood of 1922, when the Illinois River rose and practically submerged the entire town, the Sturtevant house was protected by walls of sandbags. White, trim, quaintly old-fashioned and set among shade trees, it survives as a relic of the era when palatial steamboats plied the Illinois River and Lawyer Abe Lincoln defended "Duff" Armstrong in the Beardstown courthouse.

Adobe Construction

WHEN sawmills and brickyards began to appear in Illinois the crude log cabins of the first inhabitants were supplanted by frame and brick houses designed after the architecture prevalent on the Eastern Seaboard and on Southern plantations. Since the architectural styles then current were either Georgian or Greek Revival, a good many of the first dwellings copied these styles. But whatever their design, these early homes were built of wood, stone, or brick.

An exception to this rule, however, is a two-story house built on a farm some three miles northeast of Virginia, seat of Cass County and

Historic American Buildings Survey

Andrew Cunningham House, Near Virginia, Built 1852.

one of the first settlements on the old Springfield-Beardstown road, now State Highway 125. Still in a fairly good state of preservation after almost a century of existence, this house is one of the most unusual dwellings in the state. What gives it distinction is that it is built entirely of adobe brick. It is believed to be the only adobe house in Illinois, and there are some who claim it is the only house of this type in the Midwest.

As is well known, the adobe form of construction is peculiar to the dry, sunny Southwest, where it was used extensively by the early Spanish conquerors. Curiously enough, the adobe house at Virginia was not built by anyone from New Mexico or Texas, but by a practical and resourceful Scot who had never, so far as is known, visited the Southwest.

96

That Scotsman was Andrew Cunningham. Soon after arriving in New York in 1834 he heard of the opportunities to be found on the western frontier and started for Illinois. He came westward on an Erie Canal boat, by stage, and on foot. Upon arriving at his destination he decided to set up a tannery. This required a plentiful supply of water and oak timber and these he found to his satisfaction in Cass County—at a place on Job's Creek called Sugar Grove. Here Cunningham acquired a large tract of land for a farm and built himself a small house.

The tannery was soon a thriving project. Andrew Cunningham's fortunes rose and it was then he decided to erect a more substantial house. That brought up the problem of suitable building material.

The story of how Cunningham built his adobe house in central Illinois is interestingly told in Volume 28 of the *Journal of the Illinois State Historical Society*. It was written by Lorene Martin of Virginia. After pointing out how Cunningham was "a man of great industry and resourcefulness, with a mind well stored with practical information," the author of the article gives a detailed picture of the construction of this unique house.

"Taking common mud," she writes, "and mixing it with ground tanbark, using hair scraped from hides before tanning as a binder, he molded large blocks (6 by 12 by 18 inches) and baked them in the sun. The result was satisfactory, and from these adobe bricks a substantial and well proportioned two-story house, having nine large rooms, besides two broad halls, was built. Upon completion the exterior was given a coating of cement plaster for protection against a possibly unfavorable effect of the Illinois climate. Overhanging eaves—supported by braces of ironwork beautifully designed by Mr. Cunningham himself, who had a strong artistic sense—were added for further protection against the weather and gave as well a pleasing balance to the architectural lines."

This house, we are told, was completed in 1852. In the years following, it attracted widespread attention because of its unusual construction. Despite this, however, the adobe style of house did not win popular approval in Illinois.

When he died in 1895 Andrew Cunningham left his heirs the diary of his trip to Illinois in 1835, his library, household articles, art objects, and one other reminder of him. That was a circular plot of ground in front of the adobe house which he ordered should never be touched as it contained original prairie grass—the six- to eight-foot high grass which covered the great, wide prairies of Illinois before the coming of the white man.

Hudson River Gothic

IN SELECTING ancient courthouses, covered bridges, sawmills, early taverns, and old homes of Illinois as subjects for scale drawings, draftsmen of the Historic American Buildings Survey considered the architecture of these structures as well as their historic value. This was especially true of the state's venerable dwellings. Since Illinois contains almost all of the various architectural styles that prevailed in the earlier days of the republic, the federal draftsmen included in their survey representative examples of each of these styles, chosen from among the many in all parts of the state.

A house picked for this purpose by the Survey architects stands in Paris. This central Illinois city, seat of Edgar County and a community of some nine thousand population, contains numerous fine old houses but the best known, both for its architecture and the man who built it, is this dwelling which was chosen for special study.

The Paris house thus honored is called the old Austin place. It was built in 1854, or shortly after the village of Paris was platted by Judge Albert B. Austin, long a prominent citizen of Edgar County and well-known jurist of central Illinois before and after the Civil War. In addition to his service on the bench, Judge Austin helped to organize and build the schools of Edgar County and took an active interest in the county's religious affairs. He was, furthermore, the father of ten children, eight of whom grew to maturity.

Judge Austin was born in New York State in 1808. In that state he grew up, was married, became a man of some consequence, and then, in 1852, traveled westward with his family and settled at Paris. Here his outstanding abilities were soon recognized and not long afterward he was elected clerk of the county court and, later, judge of the probate court. After his house was completed, it was widely admired for its architecture.

It was this style of architecture which attracted the attention of the government draftsmen more than three quarters of a century after the house was built. For they found it to be a good example of what is known to architectural historians as Hudson River Gothic. This style, which was popular in Judge Austin's native state during the 1840's and 1850's, is marked by pointed arches and other medieval forms.

But the Austin house, as well as those in the Hudson River Valley from which it was copied, was not built of stone or brick, which were the materials usually associated with Gothic buildings. It is a frame dwell-

Historic American Buildings Survey

Albert B. Austin House, Paris, Built 1854.

ing covered with board-and-batten siding, and its general design is like that of any other typical frame house of the Gothic Revival in America. What makes it distinctive, what sets it apart as a Gothic dwelling, is found in the scrollwork trim and ornamental detail of its exterior.

On the gables, on the east portico, and on a tall, narrow, second-story window over the portico, are evidences of the "pointed" design familiar to Americans in church architecture of the last century. The gable ends are ornamented with the tapering wooden spires that characterize the style. Traces of the earlier classic influences are found in the doorways and lintels. The house is two stories high, gable-roofed, and contains twelve rooms. There is no suggestion of the Gothic in the interior, this part being plain and conventional and having the usual fireplaces of dwellings of that era. The parlor and dining room of the house are furnished with Austin family heirlooms, such as a walnut parlor set, chests, whatnots, and an impressive Seth Thomas clock. Here, too, in old-fashioned oval frames, are faded pictures of Judge and Mrs. Austin—two persons who look intelligent, sturdy, persevering, and in general like the men and women who helped to build the Midwest.

A World Shrine

AT THE NORTHEAST corner of Eighth and Jackson streets, in the capital city of Springfield, there stands a green-shuttered, white frame house that has become a world shrine. To this central Illinois house annually come more people from all parts of the nation and the world than to any other historic shrine west of the Alleghenies. This dwelling, of course, was the home of Abraham Lincoln.

When Lincoln, who, at the time, was a tall, thirty-three-year-old Springfield lawyer, sought the services of a minister for his marriage to Mary Todd, he went to his friend, the Rev. Charles Dresser. The call was made at the minister's recently built home in Springfield. The story goes that Lincoln was so attracted by the minister's house, so pleased with its comfort, roominess, and architectural design, that a desire was born in him to own just such a home. Sixteen months later Abraham Lincoln became owner and occupant of the minister's house.

Of the thousands of visitors who come to this dwelling annually, few know the full story of the house itself. A. L. Bowen, former state director of public welfare, historian, and Lincoln scholar, gave its complete history in an address before the Lincoln Centennial Association. Entitled "A. Lincoln: His House," Mr. Bowen's address is printed in the Lincoln Centennial Association Papers for 1925.

In speaking of Lincoln's feeling for this dwelling, Mr. Bowen says: "Love and affection for this house were inseparable from his consciousness that, in all he had done in life, it expressed his greatest and chiefest achievement. It stood concretely for his triumph over poverty, want and ignorance. . . . I think it made him feel himself a man among men. He may not have been aware of any such influence at work upon him; yet the possession of this house must have afforded him a new outlook upon life."

The story of this world-famous house begins with the year 1839. That was when it was built by the Rev. Mr. Dresser. It was then only a story-and-a-half dwelling and stood on the outskirts of the city where the homes of the most influential Springfield citizens were located.

For almost two years after their marriage the Lincolns lived in a hotel, the Globe, and here their first child, Robert, was born. Then, in 1844, they moved into the Eighth Street house. This house was the only one Lincoln ever owned. The price he paid for it and the lot was $1,500 in cash. Although not mentioned in the deed, there was a $900 mortgage on the house which was cleared a few months later. In referring to this mortgage afterward, Lincoln is supposed to have said that he "reckoned he could trust the preacher that married him." Some time in the middle 1850's the house, at the suggestion of Mrs. Lincoln, was raised to a full two-story residence.

When Lincoln and his family moved to Washington in 1847—he had been elected to Congress the year before—the Eighth Street house was rented to one Cornelius Ludlum. The Lincolns returned to their dwelling a year later and remained there until the master of the house was elected President of the United States. During the years he lived in this abode—years in which three more sons came to him—Lincoln spent his time quietly and unostentatiously and there is no record of

Abraham Lincoln House, Springfield, Built 1839.

any notable social events here until he became President-elect of the United States.

When he was elected, Lincoln was formally notified of the event by a committee from Chicago and this occurred in the south parlor of the house. After the Lincolns moved to Washington in 1861 the house was rented to L. Tilton, president of the Great Western Railroad. A few years later it was rented to George H. Harlow, who later became Secretary of State for Illinois. Then, after several years' occupancy by a Dr. Gustav Wendlandt, it was rented in 1884 to O. H. Oldroyd, well-known collector of Lincolniana.

It was Oldroyd who urged the then owner of this shrine, Robert Todd Lincoln, to deed it to the state. This was done in 1887 and Oldroyd became its first official custodian. Succeeding custodians have been Herman Hofferkamp, neighbor of the Lincolns'; Albert S. Edwards, Mrs. Lincoln's nephew; Mrs. Albert S. Edwards, and Mrs. Mary Edwards Brown, the preceding custodians' daughter. The present custodian, Miss Virginia Stuart Brown, graciously carries on the tradition of hospitality set by her mother and grandmother.

As all who have visited it know, the house is well-preserved. Students of architecture note that its exterior, although plain, has touches of the Greek Revival style, which was the vogue in this country during the late 1830's. The framework of the house is of oak while the siding, trim, and flooring are of black walnut. What few nails were used in its construction—wooden pegs were mostly used—are all hand-wrought. Standing on a slight elevation, the white-painted dwelling is partly surrounded by a low brick retaining wall and a white picket fence which were ordered built by Lincoln.

No changes have been made in the interior of this twelve-room house since the Lincolns left it. Lincoln's bedroom was on the second floor, north. Since most of the original Lincoln family furniture was destroyed in the Chicago fire of 1871, when the widowed Mrs. Lincoln was living in Chicago, the house is appropriately outfitted with furniture of the Lincoln era. Some original pieces, however, are on display, including Lincoln's favorite rocking chair, a cupboard used as a bookcase, Mrs. Lincoln's sewing chair, and an original photograph of Lincoln.

Official Home of Illinois Governors

RARELY regarded as an old Illinois house, one dating from pioneer days, is the Governor's Mansion in the state capital. This is due partly to its being kept always in first-class condition and partly to the numerous additions imposed on it from time to time which have somewhat changed its original appearance. Gazing today at its white façade stand-

The Executive Mansion, Springfield, Built 1856.

ing out impressively against a beautifully landscaped background, one can hardly believe that this residence is nearly a century old.

But such it is. It was built in 1856. Among those who at intervals watched the brickmasons erecting it was Abraham Lincoln, then a lawyer and ex-congressman who was beginning to attract national attention for his political gifts. A year after the house was built, Mr. and Mrs. Lincoln were guests at a brilliant social function held here by the second executive to occupy it, Governor William H. Bissell.

The first chief executive of the state to live here was Governor Joel A. Matteson. It has been the home of every Illinois governor since 1856. Before that time, and beginning with the year 1839 when the state capital was moved from Vandalia to Springfield, the governors lived in a house at the northwest corner of Eighth Street and Capitol Avenue (then Market Street). It was a plain, two-story building and, when abandoned by the state, sold for $2,680.

"The first official act of the Illinois General Assembly looking toward the erection of a governor's mansion was approved on February 12, 1853," writes Paul M. Angle, former State Historian in charge of the Illinois State Historical Library and now director and secretary of the Chicago Historical Society. "An appropriation of $15,000 was voted for this purpose. Two years later, an additional $16,000 was voted for completion of the house. Thus, the total original cost of the Governor's Mansion was $31,000."

Topped by an imposing cupola, the Mansion was remodeled during the term of Governor Joseph W. Fifer in 1889. The cupola was removed, the roof raised to a higher pitch, and a balustraded platform built at the peak. A flagpole stands in the center of this platform. Another change made that year was the addition of the present portico. Ever since that time, the state legislature has appropriated funds at intervals for the upkeep and repair of the Governor's Mansion.

The first child born in the Governor's Mansion was Robert Oglesby, son of Governor Richard J. Oglesby, who began his first term in 1873. Another born in this house was Kühne Beveridge, who became a well-known sculptor and writer. She was a granddaughter of Governor John L. Beveridge.

The first wedding in the Mansion occurred in 1856, when Lydia Olivia, daughter of Governor Matteson, married John McGinnis, Jr. The only governor to die in the Mansion—and the first to die in office—was Governor Bissell, whose death occurred in 1860.

The Mansion is a three-story brick dwelling, white-painted and standing on a landscaped knoll not far from the Capitol. It contains twenty-eight rooms. The offices of the governor are on the ground floor. The state dining room and reception rooms are on the first floor, and the suites of bedrooms, sun parlor, and library are on the second floor. An oil portrait of Edward D. Baker, friend of Lincoln's, hangs in the state dining room. Painted by an unknown artist, it was bought by Lincoln himself and afterward presented to the state by Mrs. Lincoln.

Art Museum and Social Center

OF THE NUMEROUS historic old dwellings in Springfield, one of the oldest and most revered is the stately mansion at 801 North Fifth Street in which lived Judge Benjamin S. Edwards, member of the famous Edwards family of early Illinois. Standing in its original grove of elms and maples, its wide overhanging cornice, spacious piazza, Corinthian columns, and fanciful cupola showing signs of great age, the Edwards mansion is now the home of the Springfield Art Association.

As an art museum and center of cultural and social activities, this ancient brick residence is carrying on a role that was first given to it when Judge Edwards and his wife moved into it in 1843. They were an educated couple, fond of painting, music, literature, and all the other refinements of civilization. Among frequent guests at social events in their mansion were Abraham Lincoln and his wife, and here, too, came General U. S. Grant, Stephen A. Douglas, Senator Lyman Trumbull,

Benjamin S. Edwards House, Springfield, Built 1833.

105

Judge John Dean Caton, John Hay, Judge Sidney Breese, and other well-known figures of early Illinois.

This house, however, was not built by Judge Edwards. From a pamphlet written late in her life by Mrs. Edwards, we learn that it was erected in 1833 on a fourteen-acre tract of wooded land, then outside the town limits of Springfield. Its builder was Dr. Thomas Houghan, pioneer physician of Springfield. He must have been a man of considerable means, as the house is of imposing design and proportions, and, for its time, was probably the handsomest in that part of Illinois. The interior was, and still is, gracious and homelike, with open fireplaces in many of the rooms and the added warm glow of fine old walnut woodwork.

Ten years after building it, Dr. Houghan sold it to Judge Edwards. The judge was the youngest son of Ninian Edwards, the only governor of the Territory of Illinois, later the state's first United States senator and, subsequently, its third governor under statehood. Another son of the governor, Ninian Wirt Edwards, state representative, member of the "Long Nine" in the state assembly and Illinois' first Superintendent of Public Instruction, married a sister of Abraham Lincoln's wife.

During pre-Civil War days, when the Edwards mansion was in its prime, it was the scene of many brilliant gatherings. We are told that "legislative parties" were held on the lawn, attended by all members of the state legislature. The grove north of the house was used for numerous political meetings. One of these was addressed by Stephen A. Douglas.

Writing of President Lincoln's funeral, Mrs. Edwards said: "Our house, being on the road to the cemetery, was thrown open, our rooms were all occupied, cots being put in the library and back room even, to accommodate friends who came from Kentucky and elsewhere."

After Judge Edwards died in 1886 his widow continued to live in the mansion until her death in 1909. Here were born and reared her two daughters, Alice and Mary Stuart. After the death of Mrs. Edwards, the house was unoccupied for a number of years and then, in 1913, was presented to the Springfield Art Association by one of the Edwards daughters, Mrs. Alice Edwards Ferguson. She wanted it to stand as a memorial to her parents and, in addition, to be of service to the community.

In the hands of the Art Association members, the old Springfield landmark, now known as "Edwards Place," has been considerably restored to its former grandeur and serves not only as an art museum, but as a "period house." The rooms are enhanced with authentic furniture of the ante-bellum period.

Home of a Poet

CONSIDERABLY overshadowed by the widespread fame of the Lincoln house a few blocks away, the Vachel Lindsay home in Springfield, nonetheless, holds its own as a historic shrine, particularly as an object of veneration to literary pilgrims. It was in this attractive old dwelling, shaded in summer by great elms and maples, that Vachel Lindsay,

Vachel Lindsay House, Springfield, Built 1850's.

known in American literary history as "the tramp poet," was born, and it was here that he died fifty-two years later.

But this is not its only claim to recognition. For it has close associations with Abraham Lincoln and Mrs. Lincoln. Here both of them came often as visitors in the days before they left Springfield for Washington and here Lincoln's sister-in-law presided as chatelaine for many years. And at a later date the brooding spirit of Lincoln seemed to cling to this house, impressing the mind of the youthful Vachel Lindsay and inspiring him, when he grew to maturity, to write numerous poems on the Lincoln theme, the best known of which is "Abraham Lincoln Walks at Midnight."

Research by Paul M. Angle reveals that this house, which stands at 603 South Fifth Street (just back of the Governor's Mansion), was owned and occupied in the middle 1850's by Clark M. Smith, a leading

107

Springfield merchant. Smith is believed to have moved into this dwelling soon after his marriage to Anna Maria Todd, younger sister of Mary Todd, wife of Abraham Lincoln.

Here the Smiths lived and played important roles in the social life of ante-bellum Springfield. It was in a back room on the third floor of Smith's dry goods store, which fronted on Springfield's courthouse square, that President-elect Lincoln began writing the address he was to deliver at his inauguration in Washington. He chose this place in order to avoid the crowds who came to see him at his law office. The Smith desk on which he wrote the address is now on display in the Illinois State Historical Library in the Centennial Building in Springfield.

While the Smiths were still living in the Fifth Street house there came to Illinois from Kentucky a young doctor named Vachel Thomas Lindsay. He practiced medicine in Springfield, married an Indiana school teacher and artist named Esther Catherine Frazee in 1876, and a few years later became owner and occupant of the Smith abode on Fifth Street. Here Vachel Lindsay was born on November 10, 1879.

From Edgar Lee Masters' biography, *Vachel Lindsay A Poet in America*, we learn that when Vachel was eight or nine years old he played with his cousin, Ruby Lindsay, who lived next door to the Abraham Lincoln home on Eighth Street. The then custodian of the Lincoln home, who was fond of youngsters, often invited little Vachel and his cousin into the Lincoln house and here the future poet first became imbued with the Lincoln spirit.

When he grew to maturity, Vachel Lindsay wandered out into the world, walked up and down and across America, became famous as "the tramp poet," read, or rather chanted, his poems to farmers and college students, and then, after his marriage to Elizabeth Conner at Spokane in 1925, returned to Springfield and settled down in the house in which he was born. Here his two children were born and here he wrote many poems. And here, in 1931, he became a victim of melancholia and took his own life.

The house is still in sound condition. It is of frame construction, two stories high, and has suggestions, especially on the porch and cornices, of the Greek Revival, though the Grecian style is much modified by later influences. The interior is typical of its period, with living rooms containing windows that reach from floor to ceiling. Vachel Lindsay wrote many of his poems in the room on the second floor in the northwest corner. His final resting place is in Oak Ridge Cemetery, not far from Lincoln's tomb.

Fancy Creek Farmhouse

A FEW MILES north of Springfield there stands, in a grove of maples, a spacious old white house that has been a landmark of the region for almost a hundred years. In it lived a pioneer who played no small part in the development of Sangamon County and who was also associated with numerous historical figures of the state and nation, notably Abraham Lincoln and Stephen A. Douglas. Kept in good condition throughout its long life, this house is now occupied by the fourth generation of the same family.

Here lived, throughout the Civil War period and for many years afterward, George Power, or "Squire" Power, as he was affectionately known to his farmer neighbors and to the early citizens of Springfield. For almost twenty years he was a justice of the peace in the little settlement of Cantrall, just north of Springfield, and before him, according to tradition, Abraham Lincoln tried his first law case. The little white frame courthouse in which this case was heard now stands on the grounds of the Power home and is frequently visited by Lincoln students and devotees.

The story of Lincoln's appearance before Squire Power was told several years ago by V. Y. Dallman in his column in the *Illinois State Register*. "According to Clayton Barber [Sangamon County attorney] there is no definite record as to this first law suit," writes Dallman, "but Mr. Barber believes it was the suit involving the killing of a dog in which Lincoln defended the man with the shotgun who killed the dog! The owner of the dog insisted that the man who shot the dog should have used 'the other end of the gun,' to which Mr. Lincoln replied, 'that would have been all right if the dog had come at him with the other end.'"

It was in 1836 that Squire Power heard this suit. The courthouse in which it was heard had been built in 1829 and was the first frame dwelling in the county erected north of the Sangamon River. We are told that Lincoln, then a gangling young law student, often visited Judge Power here on his travels between New Salem and Springfield. The little courthouse, built of clapboards, contains two rooms, both of which are finished with smooth black walnut. In one of the rooms, however, the walls are papered with newspapers, now old and frayed, and among these one can read Mexican War news in the columns of the *Illinois State Register*.

In an article on Squire Power, recently written by his great-granddaughter, Virginia Reilly Glore (actress and dramatic reader), we read that "Illinois had been a state just three years when young George Power came to Sangamon County. His people had been Virginians who stopped in Kentucky for a generation. George Power was born in Fayette County, Kentucky, on February 18, 1798. In the fall of 1821 he and his young wife and baby first saw the beautiful broad sweep of the Illinois prairie. They picked a hill beside a rushing creek, with a

George Power Home, Cantrall, Built 1850's.

windbreak of timber to the north . . . black walnut trees and white oaks. Here George Power built a log cabin and thus Illinois became the home of the Power family."

An energetic young man, blond and six feet tall, George Power at this period tilled his land and dreamed of a time when he would build himself a spacious dwelling similar to those he had seen in Kentucky. He dreamed, too, of broad, cultivated acres, thoroughbred horses, blooded stock, and all the comforts of a Southern plantation. But as he dreamed, he worked. In time he prospered. Then came the Black Hawk War. He was commissioned second lieutenant of a company of mounted volunteers by Governor John Reynolds. After the war he returned to his farm on Fancy Creek and once more tilled the soil, raised cattle, and served as justice of the peace.

It was not long now until he realized his dream. Some time in the 1850's he built for himself and family a roomy, two-story house of red brick, with spacious white porches. The bricks were made by hand. His two sons, William D. and James E., were now growing up. Always hospitable, Squire Power and his wife, Nancy, entertained many prominent people here in those years and among them was Stephen A. Douglas, who had stopped overnight in 1860 after making a speech in Springfield.

The story is told that during the lean years of the Civil War, Squire Power instructed the local flour mill to give the families of soldiers whatever flour they needed, and he would pay for it. The bill came to a total of $600 and he paid it. Another story about him is that at the age of seventy-nine he "was awarded a gold-headed cane at the annual fair for the most skillful feat of horseback riding by any person over sixty." Squire Power died in 1886 at the age of eighty-eight. He was buried in a mausoleum of native limestone he had built for himself and family on the grounds of his estate.

But before he died, Squire Power was to see his own son, William, rise to prominence as a county judge in Springfield. An interesting coincidence is that Abraham Lincoln filed his last case in Sangamon County, before becoming President of the United States, in the court of County Judge William Power—just as he filed his first case before William's father, Squire Power. After the death of Squire Power, the big house in the grove of maples above Fancy Creek was occupied by the second son, James, who became a successful stock raiser.

When James Power died in 1898, the house was taken over by his son, Charles. Under his supervision, Power Farms became one of the best-known tracts in central Illinois. He then gave up active farming, moved to Springfield, and entered the office of Secretary of State Edward J. Hughes. The next occupant of the old Power homestead was— and still is—Charles' sister, June Power Reilly. She and her daughter, Virginia (now a resident of Missoula, Montana), cherish the great number of family heirlooms which adorn the house. Among these are a three-cornered walnut cupboard, a cherry wood four-poster bed, and gold-plated chandeliers.

Visitors to the Power homestead will see acres and acres of cultivated farm land and grazing cattle, a well-preserved old residence of white-painted brick, wide bluegrass lawns shaded by ancient maples, and, not far from the homestead, the little frame courthouse and the family cemetery—a cemetery where lie the remains of Squire Power's slaves whom he freed in the 1830's but who chose to remain with the family the rest of their days.

In the Spoon River Country

Major Walker who had talked
With venerable men of the revolution . . .

THESE LINES, from the opening poem in Edgar Lee Masters' book of poetic epitaphs, *Spoon River Anthology*, refer to Major Newton Walker, pioneer settler of Lewistown, early state representative, intimate friend of Abraham Lincoln's, and a commanding figure of the Spoon River country in the 1830's and '40's.

Standing today as a memorial to this man is the house in which he lived—a low, story-and-a-half brick dwelling, distinguished by corbie gables and located on the outskirts of Lewistown. It is one of Lewistown's three outstanding old houses, the other two being the ancient, grandiose mansion of Colonel Lewis W. Ross (for whom the central Illinois city was named) and the boyhood home of the poet, Edgar Lee Masters.

When Masters described Major Walker as a person who had conversed with "venerable men of the revolution," he was referring to the major's career before settling in Lewistown in 1835. A native of Virginia, where he was born in 1803, Walker was appointed a major in the Virginia militia at the age of twenty-one, and, as a military man, came into contact with Thomas Jefferson, John Randolph, James Madison, and other leaders of the American Revolution.

"Major Walker was . . . a man who already had arrived at considerable distinction when he came to Illinois," writes Mrs. Carl B. Chandler in her article, "The Spoon River Country," in the *Journal of the Illinois State Historical Society* (Vol. 14). "While yet but twenty-one, as Major in the state militia, he had been appointed to the command of the escort of Lafayette when that great man paid his memorable visit to this country in 1824, accompanying him during almost all of that triumphal trip through Virginia."

In 1834 Major Walker married Miss Eliza Simms, daughter of a respected Virginia family. Her sister, Frances, was afterward to become the wife of Colonel Ross, son of the founder of Lewistown. A year after their marriage, the Walkers came west and settled in Lewistown, the journey taking sixty days. The town in which they settled, situated just north of the Spoon River and not far from the Illinois River, had been laid out in 1822 by Ossian M. Ross, who had been granted land here by the government for his services in the War of 1812.

112

Historic American Buildings Survey

Newton Walker House, Lewistown, Built 1851.

By the time the Walkers arrived, Lewistown was the seat of Fulton County. This county, organized by Ossian Ross, was at first very large and embraced the entire northern portion of Illinois, including the future site of Chicago. The story is told that settlers of the little village of Chicago, whose log houses clustered about Fort Dearborn, had to travel to Lewistown for licenses to wed, to open taverns, or to pay their taxes.

At first, the Walkers occupied a log cabin built by Ossian Ross on the approximate site of the present Walker house. Major Walker had acquired the log house when he purchased one hundred acres of land from Ross in 1839. The date of construction of the present brick dwelling is given as 1851. This was determined by architects of the Historic American Buildings Survey.

Before his brick house was finished, however, Major Walker had achieved some renown in Fulton County and throughout central Illinois as the designer and builder of the county's third courthouse—an impressive Greek Revival edifice, completed in 1838, that became the pride of Lewistown.

In it Abraham Lincoln, Robert Ingersoll, and Edward Dickinson Baker appeared as lawyers and here sat Stephen A. Douglas as a judge.

This fine courthouse, with its columns and portico, was mysteriously burned to the ground on a December night in 1894. In that year Major Walker was ninety-one years old and was still living in his brick abode on the outskirts of town. Legend says the fire was started by an incendiary in a bitter county seat "war" between Lewistown and near-by Canton. But this was never legally proved.

There is a humorous legend in Lewistown to the effect that Major Walker, while supervising the building of the courthouse, constructed a large bobsled inside the building. When the sled was completed, it was discovered there was no way to get it outside the courthouse, which had been finished about the same time. The townspeople laughed at Major Walker's dilemma. But the major was not disturbed. He simply took the sled apart and set it up again outside the courthouse.

Of particular interest to historians and Lincoln devotees is the fact that Major Walker was Lincoln's closest friend in Lewistown. The Major first met the future President when he and Lincoln were members of the General Assembly in the old State Capitol at Vandalia. On his visits to Lewistown, Lincoln stopped in Major Walker's brick house, and the story is told that Major Walker often played his fiddle for Abe Lincoln in exchange for stories from the lanky Springfield lawyer.

It was in this house that Lincoln ate his last dinner, and made his last appearance, in Lewistown. This was when he delivered a speech from the portico of the old courthouse on August 17, 1858, in answer to an address delivered the day before by Stephen A. Douglas at near-by Proctor's Grove. That evening Lincoln was a dinner guest in Major Walker's house, and the following morning the Major drove Lincoln to a railroad station thirty-two miles away.

Major Walker lived in the brick house until his death in 1897. The dwelling afterward was acquired by a number of successive owners. There have been few changes made in the house since it was originally built almost a hundred years ago. Standing there under the great old trees of Lewistown, its white brick walls and frame porch showing signs of age, the Walker house is often visited by historically minded sightseers, Lincoln scholars, and devoted readers of the works of Edgar Lee Masters.

A distinctive feature of this house is found in the buttressed gable ends of brick masonry. The interior is finished in plaster and wallpaper, with hard maple flooring and cherry wood trim. The rooms are comfortable, with little ornamentation. Surrounding the house is a small park dedicated to the memory of the man who entertained Lincoln here with his fiddle and his hospitality.

A Poet's Boyhood Home

ILLINOIS has numerous old dwellings which have become literary land-marks because of their association with noted writers. Not least of these is the boyhood home of the poet, Edgar Lee Masters, at Peters-burg, an old town on the banks of the Sangamon River. A modest cottage, with little architectural appeal, this house is frequently visited by devotees of Masters' widely read *Spoon River Anthology*, as well as by literary scholars in general.

In her article, "The Spoon River Country," Josephine Craven Chandler (now Mrs. Robert C. Horner) says that "It was here [in Peters-burg] that Masters spent most of those early years before he moved to Lewistown; here he came to know personally, and through the infinite resources of anecdote and familar allusion, that group of characters which are among the most benign and ennobling of the collection [in the *Spoon River Anthology*]; and here he came beneath the spell of those two men who were to prove, immediate family influences aside, the most constant sources of inspiration in his life and art—his grandfather, Mr. Squire D. Masters, and Abraham Lincoln."

Edgar Lee Masters House, Petersburg, Built 1870's.

It was not that Edgar Lee Masters knew Lincoln personally, for the Civil War President was dead four years before the poet was born. What Mrs. Horner means is that Masters grew up in the Lincoln country, in a town surveyed by Lincoln and among people who knew Lincoln, and that as a result the impressionable young boy was early imbued with the Lincoln tradition. As a child, Masters remembered seeing, in the Petersburg courthouse square, such men as Mentor Graham, William H. Herndon, and others who had been associates of the martyred President.

When the Masters family moved into its little white house in Petersburg some time in the early 1870's, the poet was a lad of about three years old. At that time his father, Hardin Wallace Masters, had but recently been elected state's attorney of the county in which they lived, Menard. The house came to the new state's attorney as a gift from his father, Squire Masters, who was a well-to-do farmer living some miles outside Petersburg.

Although Illinois was the state of his ancestors and the state in which he was reared and to which he devoted most of his writings, Edgar Lee Masters was not born in the Prairie State. His birth occurred at Garnett, Kansas, on August 23, 1869, where his parents had moved from Illinois a year or two earlier. A young lawyer, Hardin Masters had gone to Kansas in search of opportunities. Not finding them, he returned to Petersburg with his family.

After an attempt at farming near the village of Atterberry, Hardin Masters was prevailed on to become a candidate for state's attorney. He accepted, was elected, and moved into the Petersburg house. Here his family lived until 1880. In that year they moved to Lewistown, in Fulton County near the Spoon River. When this move was made Edgar Lee Masters was eleven years old. It was at Lewistown he grew to maturity and studied law in his father's office. He afterward went to Chicago, engaged in the practice of law, wrote his renowned *Spoon River Anthology*, and became one of America's foremost poets.

A goodly portion of his boyhood days in the Petersburg house is described by Masters in his autobiography, *Across Spoon River*. "This was a small house and common enough; but there was a large yard and trees and a barn," he writes. "Later my father built an addition to the house; but it had neither water save from a well nor heat save from stoves. And in winter it was cold as the arctic."

That house, whose exact address is 528 Monroe Street, is still in good condition. Standing next to a school on the slope of a hill above Petersburg, it is not greatly different from hundreds of other old frame dwellings of this Sangamon River town.

Where Lincoln and Douglas Agreed

*In the southwest room of this house on the night of July 29, 1858,
Abraham Lincoln and Stephen A. Douglas made formal agreement to
hold joint debate in Illinois.*

THIS IS the message on a bronze marker at the front entrance of a
small white-painted, green-shuttered cottage in Bement, located just
across the railroad tracks from the city's business section. A marked
arrow on state highway 105, which enters the town from the north, points
eastward to the dwelling. In front of it hangs a flag on a tall pole.

This house is one of Piatt County's principal sights. For in the

Historic American Buildings Survey

Francis E. Bryant House, Bement, Built 1856.

prim, tiny parlor of this cottage occurred the event which, as has been
said, "proved to be a large contributing factor in making Lincoln President of the United States."

The man who was host to the two distinguished guests on that mo-
mentous occasion was Francis E. Bryant, one of the "fathers" of Bement,
an early banker of the town and a cousin of the poet, William Cullen
Bryant. He was also an intimate friend of Stephen A. Douglas, and it

was this friendship which brought about the appearance of Abraham Lincoln in his home. Bryant was to live long enough to see Lincoln become a greater figure in history than Douglas.

Coming westward to Chicago in the early 1850's, Francis E. Bryant did not stay long in the young city by the lake. It is said he could "see no future" in Chicago. So he headed toward central Illinois and settled at Bement in 1856. That same year he built the frame cottage which has become one of the chief points of interest to sightseers in that part of the state. He and his wife and family lived here many years and were highly esteemed by the townsfolk of Bement.

The story of the event which made this cottage famous goes back to a July day in 1858 when Senator Douglas was scheduled to speak in near-by Monticello, county seat of Piatt County. He and his wife arrived earlier in Bement and were the house guests of Mr. and Mrs. Bryant. On their way to Monticello in a carriage, the Douglases and Bryants met a prairie schooner. In it were Lincoln and his friends. Lincoln jumped out of the wagon and greeted Senator Douglas.

On the prairie road that day Lincoln asked Douglas where they could meet to discuss a series of joint debates. At this point the Bryants invited the two political rivals to confer that evening in their Bement home. This invitation was accepted and Lincoln and Douglas talked for two hours in the Bryant parlor. The following day Douglas wrote a letter to Lincoln on the Bryants' marble-topped table, accepting Lincoln's challenge to the joint debates.

The room in which this conference took place has been preserved almost intact. One of the principal exhibits is the walnut chair in which Lincoln sat. After his assassination Francis Bryant draped the chair with crepe and a small American flag. These are still on it. On the wall above the chair are oval-framed portraits of Mr. and Mrs. Bryant. Here, also, is the marble-topped table at which Lincoln and Douglas sat, as well as the chairs, whatnot, divan, and other articles of furniture dating from the night of the historic meeting.

The cottage is small, gable-roofed, and with a porch over the front entrance. In 1925, on the sixty-seventh anniversary of the event that occurred in it, the house was presented to Bement by its owner, the late J. F. Sprague, grandson of Francis E. Bryant, and mayor of Bement. "This house, set apart to the memory of the immortal Lincoln and his friend, the illustrious Douglas," said Mayor Sprague at the presentation ceremonies, "will be kept open to the public, free, so long as it endures." More recently (on July 29, 1947) the house became a state shrine.

On the University of Illinois Campus

A LANDMARK familiar to thousands who have been graduated from the University of Illinois is the small, old-fashioned private dwelling, shaded by several maples and lindens, which stands on the south campus of the Urbana seat of learning. Occupying an isolated position on the broad, open green of the campus, this house of plain domestic architecture is in sharp contrast to the Georgian façades of distant university buildings. It is a little dwelling that has the distinction of being the oldest edifice on the Urbana campus.

Both faculty and students regard it as something of a shrine and identify it as the "Mumford House." This name was given it because of the long residence here of the late Herbert W. Mumford, dean of the university's college of argiculture and nationally known farm marketing expert whose program for livestock market quotations has been adopted

Herbert W. Mumford House, Urbana, Built 1870.

119

throughout the Midwest. Dean Mumford and his family occupied this dwelling for more than thirty years.

Before that time it was the home of several earlier deans of the college of agriculture. Its first occupant was a man who might be considered one of the "fathers" of the University of Illinois. He was Thomas J. Burrill, who joined the university when it was founded in 1868 and who, as acting regent from 1891 to 1894, secured large appropriations from Governor John P. Altgeld and the state legislature which put the institution on a sound footing and widened its scope of activities.

The little gray house on the campus was built in 1870, and when Professor Burrill and his family moved into it the dwelling was known as "The Farm House." The university catalogue for 1871-72 describes it thus: "The Farm House, recently built on the horticultural grounds, is designed to afford a fair model for a farmer's house. It is tasteful in appearance, economical in cost, and compact and convenient."

Professor Burrill lived in the Farm House only a few years. It was afterward occupied by Professor George E. Morrow, who helped to found the university's agricultural experiment station and who became dean of the college of agriculture. Another dean of the same college who lived in the little house was Professor Eugene Davenport.

After Dean Davenport's retirement in 1902, the dwelling became the home of Professor Mumford and his family. At that time Professor Mumford was head of the university's animal husbandry department.

In the many years Dean Mumford lived in the little gray house, his circle of friends and associates widened and here he and Mrs. Mumford entertained many distinguished scholars, scientists, and leaders in agricultural and educational fields. Dean Mumford died in 1938.

If the little house on the campus was long known as a residence of agricultural experts, it is no less well known today as a dwelling place of nationally famous artists. For here, each year, resides the university's visiting professor of art—some noted artist sent to the campus by the Carnegie Foundation. A new artist is sent each year. While in residence, the visiting artist maintains "open house" in Mumford House for art students and the art school faculty.

The first artist to occupy the house was Dale Nichols, who came in 1939. While living here he did an effective water color of Mumford House, showing it in a midwinter setting.

Of frame construction and with a gable roof, Mumford House is as sound today as when it was built. All rooms are light and comfortable and the parlor, now a studio, is heated by a spacious fireplace. The stairway in the center of the house has a fine walnut balustrade.

Decatur Art Institute

FEW COMMUNITIES in Illinois are more closely associated with the name of one man than is Decatur, that energetic city of railroad shops, university buildings, and farmers' banks on the bluffs above the Sangamon River. Although Abraham Lincoln's name was early identified with this city, the Civil War President having lived a few miles west of it when he was young, any mention of Decatur today usually brings up the name of James Millikin and the institution he founded, James Millikin University.

This university, with its stately buildings on an attractive, rolling campus, stands as a great memorial to its founder. Several other memorials to this distinguished Illinoisan also survive and among these may be mentioned the Millikin National Bank, whose seven-story building is one of the sights of downtown Decatur. But of much greater interest than any of these as a reminder of the life of James Millikin is the house in which he lived—a house that has become almost as well known throughout Illinois as the university founded by its master.

This imposing old residence houses an art museum that is the equal of any in Illinois outside of Chicago. Several years ago, title to the mansion and park-like grounds on which it stands was transferred to the board of managers of James Millikin University. The board appointed a committee, headed by W. R. McGaughey, president of the Millikin National Bank, to maintain the old landmark and continue operating it as an art museum. It is known as the Decatur Art Institute.

As much of an exhibit as anything it shelters is the dwelling itself. If one were searching for a typical mansion of the 1870's none better could be found than the Millikin home. Two and a half stories high and built of red brick, this house has such characteristics of a late Victorian residence as tall, narrow windows with white-stone caps; tall, spacious verandas with fanciful wood trim; wide stone steps; a low-pitched mansard roof, and, that most distinguishing characteristic of all, the mansarded cupola dominating the façade and decorated with bull's-eye windows and an ornate cast-iron cresting.

These features are plainly visible during the winter months, but in summer the ancient mansion is almost hidden by the leaves of great old elms, oaks, lindens, and other trees which shade a well-kept lawn. The house stands in the center of a block-square plot of ground at the northeast corner of Main and Pine streets, or halfway between the Decatur business district and James Millikin University.

James Millikin House, Decatur, Built 1876.

From a historical book published by the Millikin National Bank, we learn that the Millikin residence was built in 1876. At that time James Millikin was the leading citizen of Decatur. He had acquired the land on which his mansion was built some fifteen years earlier from Captain David Allen, paying $2,200 for it. The residence originally cost $18,000 to build, but later improvements in the interior cost an additional $18,000. When completed it was considered one of the most impressive residences in its part of the state.

Here James Millikin reigned as the wealthiest citizen of Decatur. When he first came to Illinois, however, Millikin was not rich. He was born of Scotch Presbyterian parents at Clarkstown (now Ten Mile), Pennsylvania, on August 2, 1827. His father was a farmer. It is recorded that in young manhood James Millikin and a neighbor boy drove a herd of steers to New York City, winding up their trip by driving the animals down Broadway. He subsequently entered Washington College (now Washington and Jefferson College) at Washington, Pennsylvania.

"It was while attending Washington College," says the bank's history, "that his sympathies were aroused by the struggles of boys to secure funds enough to meet expenses and to overcome the inadequacy of their preparation for the classes they entered. Then and there, only twenty years of age, he made a vow that if ever he amassed a fortune he would found an institution of learning in which all classes of youth could secure an education fitting them for any occupation they might desire to enter. This was finally fulfilled in 1901 in the James Millikin University."

After completing his studies at Washington College, young Millikin again took up the business of being a drover, but this time his steps were turned toward the western prairies. He felt that great opportunities lay in that direction. So in 1849 he and his father drove a flock of sheep into Indiana, selling it at a good profit and returning to their Pennsylvania home. The following year young Millikin drove another flock westward, selling it this time at Danville, Illinois.

He continued in this business at Danville, making more and more profits, and then enlarged his activities to include cattle. "His large flocks and herds," says the bank's historical work, "gave him great prominence as a breeder of fine stock. He won six silver medal spoons which bear the stamp of the 'Illinois State Fair of 1857.' He has been called the 'first cattle king of the Prairie State.' . . . He at one time had 10,000 sheep, which grazed over a radius of twenty miles."

All during this time Millikin had been buying tracts of land in Illinois. The present city of Bement stands on land he originally owned. He later sold much of his land with profit, came to Decatur in 1856, entered the real-estate business, and then sold his livestock holdings. He was then one of the wealthiest men in Decatur. He decided to enter the banking field and established his bank in 1860.

Sixteen years later he built his residence at Main and Pine streets. And that house, with its many lofty, walnut-paneled rooms and ornate marble fireplaces, is still standing as an eloquent, if old-fashioned, reminder of the man who gave back to the city of Decatur almost as much money as he made in it. Here he was living at the time of his death in 1909. His widow, Mrs. Anna B. Millikin, occupied the residence until her own death in 1913. In her will she provided for use of the mansion as a museum of art.

Part III, Northern Illinois

With the opening of the Erie Canal in 1825 and the building of the first railroad out of Chicago in 1848, a greater flood than ever of homeseekers from the East came to Illinois, taking up land especially in the northern part of the state. Chicago became the gateway to a fertile, rolling prairie country. Before long, railroad trains were bringing the sons and daughters of foreign lands, sturdy people seeking homes in the New World. They, like the Easterners who preceded them, laid out farms or helped to make villages into towns, towns into cities. And a descendant of Welsh pioneers, Frank Lloyd Wright, settled in the metropolis at the foot of Lake Michigan and gave the world an architecture that is as expressive of the twentieth century as Gothic was of the twelfth.

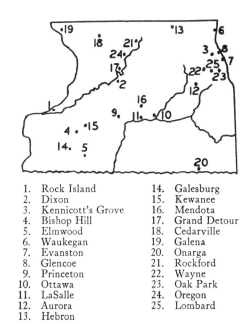

1.	Rock Island	14.	Galesburg
2.	Dixon	15.	Kewanee
3.	Kennicott's Grove	16.	Mendota
4.	Bishop Hill	17.	Grand Detour
5.	Elmwood	18.	Cedarville
6.	Waukegan	19.	Galena
7.	Evanston	20.	Onarga
8.	Glencoe	21.	Rockford
9.	Princeton	22.	Wayne
10.	Ottawa	23.	Oak Park
11.	LaSalle	24.	Oregon
12.	Aurora	25.	Lombard
13.	Hebron		

On an Island in the Mississippi

SOMEWHAT lost sight of among the numerous stone buildings of the United States Army arsenal which surround it, the old Colonel George Davenport house on Rock Island, in the Mississippi River, is one of the oldest residential landmarks of northern Illinois. Located at the west end of the tree-shaded and landscaped arsenal grounds, this ancient frame dwelling stands as a reminder of the man who, after playing an important role in the development of this region, came to a tragic end in his island abode.

Colonel Davenport built his residence in 1833, following the close of the Black Hawk War. He had served in that war as assistant quarter-

George Davenport House, Rock Island, Built 1833.

master general, an appointment he received from Governor John Reynolds. Comfortably settled in his Rock Island home, Colonel Davenport continued his public career and helped to develop this part of the Mississippi Valley. Two years after his house was completed he and a group of associates bought land across the river in Iowa and laid out a town, which was named in honor of the colonel. This is the present-day city of Davenport, Iowa.

The frame house in which Colonel Davenport was living at this time was not, however, his first dwelling on Rock Island. He had originally

126

lived in a double log cabin he built soon after arriving here in 1816. This was the first home in what was to become Rock Island County. Around this cabin a little settlement grew and it became known as Rock Island Village. A few years later the government established a post office here and Davenport was appointed the first postmaster.

A native of England, where he was born in 1783, Davenport followed the sea in his youth, arrived in New York in 1804, enlisted in the Army, served in the War of 1812, and came west at the close of that war. A few years later he was appointed head of the commissary for a new fort the government had built on Rock Island. It was called Fort Armstrong. He held this position only a year, however, giving it up to become an Indian trader both in the Illinois and Iowa country.

It was as a trader that Davenport built his log house outside the fort. Here, in 1819, the first religious service of the region was held. Here, too, George Davenport welcomed Russell Farnham, explorer, world traveler, and fur trader. The two formed a partnership and built a house on the mainland opposite Rock Island. Around it a village grew called Farnhamsburg. It was from this village that the present city of Rock Island sprang. About this time Davenport and Farnham became members of the American Fur Company, headed by John Jacob Astor, and from then on the two prospered.

There followed the construction of Davenport's frame house on the island. "Early photographs of the house," writes Architect Earl H. Reed for the Historic American Buildings Survey, "show it to have been of a highly developed type for the Midwest, with well proportioned side and rear wings, one of the former having perhaps served as an office.

"Davenport, who was a man of broad culture, traveled widely throughout the East and South and his familiarity with the finest Colonial and post-Colonial traditions shows in the architectural lines of his house. Its good proportions, skillful assemblage of tasteful detail and the exterior chimneys, make the Davenport house uniquely interesting."

In 1845, on the Fourth of July, Colonel Davenport's family went to the mainland for an Independence Day celebration. The master of the house remained home alone. Later in the day a band of river ruffians forced their way into the house with the intention of robbing Colonel Davenport. The colonel was brutally murdered and thus was brought to a tragic end the career of a man who helped to found that great metropolitan area on the upper Mississippi known as the "Quad Cities."

Cabin on the Rock River

ON THE RUSTIC, pine-shaded estate of the late Charles R. Walgreen at Dixon there stands an ancient, well-preserved log cabin that is one of the noteworthy historic landmarks of northern Illinois and the Rock River country. It has been standing there for over a century and is associated with more famous people of the state and nation than perhaps any other dwelling in that part of Illinois. And this association continues, for it now serves as the kitchen and dining room of the Walgreen guest house where well-known social and artistic personages are entertained.

Throughout the scenic and historic Rock River country this dwelling is known as the Governor Charters cabin. It dates from the earliest beginnings of white civilization in northern Illinois and stands as a lone survivor of many log dwellings that once dotted the wilderness in pioneer days. Near it is situated a venerable barn, built a year later than the cabin, and both cabin and barn have been restored by the Walgreen family and converted into living quarters which are veritable museums of pioneer Americana.

The estate, called "Hazelwood," on which the cabin stands is not of recent origin. On the contrary, estate and cabin came into being at the same time, and from the very beginning the estate was called Hazelwood. It is one of the oldest and best known of the many estates that in later years grew up on both banks of the picturesque Rock River.

The one-story log cabin, now partly covered by morning-glory vines and arched over by stately evergreens, was built in 1837 by Samuel M. Charters, brother of the man who afterward made it famous. At that time the Rock River country was just subsiding from the Black Hawk War scare and John Dixon was operating a ferry at the place where later the city of Dixon was to be established. At the request of his brother, who waited in New York, Samuel Charters came west in 1837, laid claim to 640 acres of land just north of what was later to become Dixon, and built this log cabin.

A year later the brother arrived. He was Alexander Charters, who became known in Illinois history as "Governor" Charters. Since the 640-acre tract was laid claim to in his name, he immediately settled on his land, living in the log cabin built for him by Samuel. Planning to set up an estate, he called his tract Hazelwood and began to improve it.

Alexander Charters won the friendship of the early settlers at Dixon's Ferry and the surrounding countryside. They liked him because of his hearty ways, his hospitality, his intelligence, and his education. Not long afterward Alexander built a big frame manor house a short distance from the cabin and in this house he entertained and lived the remainder of his days. As the proprietor of an estate and manor house, he was affectionately called "Governor" Charters.

From a historical sketch, "One Hundred Years at Hazelwood," written by the late Frank E. Stevens when the Walgreens observed the one-hundredth anniversary of the estate in 1937, we learn that among

Alexander Charters House, Dixon, Built 1837.

the famous people entertained at Hazelwood by "Governor" Charters were Abraham Lincoln, Stephen A. Douglas, William Cullen Bryant, General Philip Kearney, Margaret Fuller, John Quincy Adams, and Bayard Taylor.

"Governor" Charters died at Hazelwood in 1878 at the age of seventy-eight. Later the estate was acquired by Charles H. Hughes, banker and state senator. Subsequently, the old manor house was destroyed in a fire. But the log cabin and the barn remained. Then, in 1929, the estate and buildings were bought by Charles R. Walgreen, who, as a youth in Dixon, had admired the grounds of Hazelwood when he and his companions were fishing in the Rock River.

When the Walgreens acquired this historic estate, it was badly run down. But under the careful supervision of Mrs. Walgreen, who is a competent horticulturist as well as an antiquarian and student of Illinois history, the estate was restored and is now one of the beauty spots of the Rock River Valley.

Literary Settlement

SOME twenty miles northwest of Chicago, on a slight ridge shaded by oaks, elms, and a few ancient pines, stands a scattered settlement known as Kennicott's Grove. Founded more than a century ago, this settlement, located in Northfield Township, near Milwaukee and Lake avenues, is of importance today because of its association with more well-known writers, editors, and naturalists than any other similar community in Illinois. And as a result of this association, Kennicott's Grove has been the locale of numerous outstanding books, both of fiction and nonfiction.

Among the dozen or so venerable dwellings constituting "The Grove," most of which are occupied by descendants of the founder of the settlement and of his brothers, the oldest is the Jonathan Kennicott house. It was built in 1845. The man who erected it was the father of the founder of Kennicott's Grove. But this was not the first house in the settlement. That was built in 1836 by the settlement's founder—a log house which no longer stands. Because it is now the oldest, the Jonathan Kennicott dwelling is looked on with some reverence by both natives and visitors at the Grove. They recall that timbers for its construction were floated down the Des Plaines River from Half Day, where one of Jonathan's sons, Hiram, had started a sawmill in 1840.

If this house did not belong to the man who established the Grove, it nonetheless sheltered him on almost daily visits he made here during most of his mature life. This man was Dr. John A. Kennicott, known in his time as "The Old Doctor." He was not only a pioneer practicing physician, horticulturist, editor, and one of the organizers of the land-grant college system in America but he was also the father of Robert Kennicott, early Illinois naturalist, Arctic explorer, and first director of the Chicago Academy of Sciences. It was at the Grove that Dr. Kennicott established an extensive nursery that is still in existence.

In his biography of John S. Wright, founder of *The Prairie Farmer*, Lloyd Lewis writes: "Destined to become more famous than all the Kennicotts was Robert, who was a baby of one year when his father, 'The Old Doctor,' started establishing the farm and orchard which, known as 'The Grove,' was to become famous for its view, its rare and beautiful flowers, and its sweeps of fruit trees and berry bushes. Humble though the farmhouse was, it was celebrated for its hospitality. A drive out to the Grove was in the 1840's and '50's 'the' thing to do of a Sunday afternoon in the 'refined' social circles of Chicago."

130

Jonathan Kennicott House, Kennicott's Grove, Built 1845.

Although it is unfortunate that "The Old Doctor's" farmhouse is gone, the Jonathan Kennicott abode remains as a link with the earliest days of the Grove. After Jonathan's death, the house was occupied by his widow, Jean McMillan Kennicott, and her daughters, Avis, Delia, and Emma. The daughters remained unmarried and, in the family as well as throughout the countryside, were known as "the good aunts." The old Jonathan Kennicott house—a frame, L-shaped abode originally designed in the Greek Revival style—is now (1948) owned by Jonathan's great-great-grandson, J. Kennicott.

The second oldest house at the Grove is the picturesque, gabled dwelling of board-and-batten construction into which "The Old Doctor" and his family moved from their rambling log house in 1856. Afterward, it was for many years the home of the late Edward S. Beck, associate editor of *The Chicago Tribune*, who had married into the family. It is now the home of Hiram Kennicott, grand-nephew of "The Old Doctor." The third oldest house at the Grove was built by "The Old Doctor's" son, Amasa, in 1875, and is occupied by Amasa's son, Walter, who still carries on the horticultural pursuits of his father and grandfather.

Another grandson of "The Old Doctor" is Leigh Reilly onetime editor of the old *Chicago Evening Post*, who lives in retirement at the Grove. No longer standing in the settlement is the homestead of Dr. William Kennicott, a pioneer Chicago dentist and son of Jonathan Kennicott. Another son of the latter, Dr. J. Asa Kennicott, also achieved success as a dentist in Chicago, and his beautiful home "Kenwood," which stood at what is now 48th Street and Dorchester Avenue, in Chicago, gave the name to that section of the city's South Side.

With the marriage in 1923 of Donald Culross Peattie to Louise Redfield, great-granddaughter of "The Old Doctor," the settlement on the ridge entered a more distinctively literary phase. For both Mr. Peattie, who was born in Chicago, and Miss Redfield, who was born at the Grove, are writers of national reputation. And they spent many summers at the Grove, studying the natural, as well as human, history of the place.

In this century-old setting, too, lived and wrote Mrs. Peattie's brother, Professor Robert Redfield, of the University of Chicago, a widely known anthropologist. Another who came often to the Grove was Peattie's brother, Roderick Peattie, noted geographer and writer. And the Grove was the setting of two noteworthy books, Peattie's *A Prairie Grove*, and Louise Redfield Peattie's *American Acres*—two books which poetically present the natural and human history of a grove on the spacious Illinois prairie.

Early Communistic Community

Farthest west, but still to the south of the park, are three large brick structures faced with cement. Square, and three stories high, they are unlike any houses to be seen in correspondingly small towns. One of these was the hotel, each of the others, identical in arrangement, provided living quarters for several families, and thus they present, as do many of the other buildings, an early form of the modern apartment house.

THESE WORDS, appearing in an article by Margaret E. Jacobson in the *Journal of the Illinois State Historical Society* (Vol. 34), describe the few remaining dwellings of the Bishop Hill Colony, pioneer religious-communistic community founded on the Illinois prairie by Swedish immigrants. Some eighteen miles west of Kewanee, this colony attempted to be a utopia in the New World similar to the colonies established by the French at Nauvoo and by the English at Albion.

In recognition of the historical significance of the spot, the state of

Historic American Buildings Survey

Bishop Hill Colony House, Bishop Hill, Built 1840's.

133

Illinois has placed a bronze marker on highway 34 at the intersection of the road that leads to Bishop Hill. It reads: "At Bishop Hill, two miles north of here, Eric Jansen and Jonas Olson founded a colony of Swedish religious dissenters in 1846. Organized on communistic lines, the colony at one time had 1,100 members and property worth a million dollars. Dissolution and the end of the venture came in 1862."

Now shaded by great old elms, walnuts, and maples that completely arch its streets, Bishop Hill Colony still retains most of its principal houses and public buildings, although their great age is apparent. Here is the Steeple Building, built in 1854 and containing a clock in its tower that has been running continuously since it was constructed in 1859. Here, too, are the Old Colony Church, the bakery and brewery buildings, cheese factory, hospital, and Bishop Hill Cemetery.

Gone, however, is "Big Brick," which was a four-story brick communal dwelling built in 1848-1851. It had ninety-six rooms. The kitchen and dining hall were in the basement. This building was destroyed by fire in 1928 and its site is occupied by a ball park. Just east of this is Old Colony Church, a two-story frame edifice built in 1848.

"The settlement," wrote Miss Jacobson, "was a Christian communistic organization, so property, responsibility, and work were shared. Starting with sixty acres, the project accumulated a 'balance stock on hand' of $770,630.94, according to the treasurer's report in the annual statement of the Board of Trustees on January 9, 1860."

It is recorded that the colonists worked eighteen hours a day in the fields. Women labored side by side with the men. All ate their meals in the dining halls of the various communal houses in which they lived. Clothing was furnished from a community storehouse. Among the principal products of Bishop Hill during its heyday were linen, made from flax grown by the colonists, and broomcorn, which was exported in large quantities.

At the peak of its existence, however, dissension broke out in Bishop Hill. This break led to the murder of Eric Jansen in 1850. His widow became head of the colony but subsequently she, too, met opposition and soon was ousted from office. Affairs went from bad to worse and in time the colony lost its original identity. Today, Bishop Hill is a state park and descendants of the Swedish colonists live near by.

Although there are few firsthand, written accounts of life at Bishop Hill, an unusual record of existence in the colony survives in the collection of paintings displayed in Old Colony Church. These paintings are the work of one of the colonists, Olaf Krans, who is acclaimed by art critics as an outstanding American "primitive" painter.

Birthplace of a Sculptor

ALMOST within sight of "The Pioneers," that impressive bronze statue which has brought considerable fame to the little Illinois city of Elmwood, some twenty miles west of Peoria, stands a small, white-painted old house that is as much revered by both townspeople and Illinoisans in general as the statue itself. This is because the two are linked. For it was in this unpretentious frame dwelling that the man

Illinois Writers' Project

Lorado Taft House, Elmwood, Built 1850's.

who designed the statue was born and spent his boyhood days. That man was the late Lorado Taft.

There are two events now observed annually in Elmwood. One is the Fall Festival, a three-day affair which attracts farmers from all parts of Peoria County. The other is the yearly celebration of the birthday anniversary of Elmwood's most illustrious son, Lorado Taft. And on the day of this latter-named event, the Taft birthplace becomes a center of attention, visited by school children, art lovers, and just plain Elmwood folks proud of the man who, as one of them once said, "put our city on the map."

Local residents are interested in the house for other reasons, too. For one thing, it was the home of Taft's father, an esteemed pioneer teacher of Peoria County who helped bring culture into a raw, rough-and-tumble frontier settlement. Another reason is that it attracts

135

architectural students as a good example of the Greek Revival style in early American house design.

The day set aside in Elmwood for the annual Taft birthday observance is April 29. It was on that day, in the year 1860, that Lorado Taft was born in the modest little house a short distance from the public square. At that time Elmwood was but a cluster of dwellings and was not incorporated as a village until seven years later. Today, it is a thriving coal-mining center with more than a thousand population.

In the years before the Civil War, the sculptor's father, Professor Don Carlos Taft, taught school in Elmwood township. "A few scattered district schools were established earlier in the history of the township," says an old Peoria County history, "but the founding of the Elmwood Academy, in 1855, marked the beginning of a literary and educational prestige which has never abated. Professor Don Carlos Taft and Miss Anna M. Somers were the tutors in its early years, and the school acquired a renown and enjoyed a patronage extending over a wide scope of country."

As a boy in the small L-shaped Elmwood house, a plain but tastefully designed home that contained comfortable rooms lined with books, Lorado Taft was tutored by his parents and given a sound foundation for his future career. The family lived here during the Civil War years and then, when Lorado was twelve, moved to Urbana where the elder Taft became a professor of geology in the University of Illinois.

After studying at the University of Illinois, and later at the École des Beaux Arts in Paris, Lorado Taft returned to his native state, established a studio in Chicago, and began the career that brought him national fame. In addition to "The Pioneers," some of his other principal works are the "Fountain of Time" and the "Fountain of the Great Lakes" in Chicago, the "Black Hawk" statue at Oregon, Illinois, and the Lincoln statue at Urbana.

A proud moment in Lorado Taft's life was the day in 1928 when he was present at the unveiling of "The Pioneers" in Elmwood and at a reception in his boyhood home afterward. The ten-foot bronze statuary group, conceived as a tribute to his father and mother and other Illinois pioneers, was unveiled by his daughter, Emily, now the wife of Illinois' Senator-elect Paul H. Douglas of Chicago. The principal speaker was Taft's brother-in-law, Hamlin Garland, the Midwest author. Lorado Taft died in 1936 and his ashes were scattered over a plot of ground in Elmwood Cemetery—a spot now marked by one of his most effective sculptural pieces, "Memory."

Classical Masterpiece

SOME YEARS AGO a national magazine of wide circulation published a photograph of the old Swartout house in Waukegan, pointing out that it was a distinctive example of the Greek Revival style of architecture in America. This attention was well merited, for the Swartout house has long been admired by architects for its pure classic lines. It is an object of interest, too, to historical students. Built a century ago, this dwelling has associations with the early history of northern Illinois and that region north of Chicago known as the North Shore.

The man who erected the house was John H. Swartout, early settler of Lake County. He first arrived in Waukegan when that industrious North Shore city was a hamlet of log houses known as Little Fort, so named because of a French outpost which occupied the site in the eighteenth century. In the year 1846, when the U. S. government designated Little Fort as a port of entry, we find John H. Swartout one of the important citizens of the pioneer community, particularly in the religious field.

In that year he is recorded as having been one of a small group of

John H. Swartout House, Waukegan, Built 1847.

137

residents of Little Fort who banded together to organize a church of the American Baptist Mission Society. This society had sent out the Rev. Peter Freeman to establish a church in the North Shore settlement and engage in missionary work. He found a responsive co-worker in John H. Swartout, who was then a man of some means in the settlement.

Under Swartout's leadership, eleven citizens met in the Congregational Church building, which then stood on Utica Street, and formally established a church of the Baptist faith.

The first baptisms of this church were held in the Little Fort River at a point where the Chicago & North Western railroad tracks are now located. In time the congregation, again under the leadership of John Swartout, brought about the construction of a church edifice. It was a building thirty feet long by twenty-two feet wide, which stood on North Genessee Street. Here the Rev. Mr. Freeman preached to an ever-growing congregation and here John Swartout wielded strong influence in the religious growth of Little Fort.

When John Swartout built his house in 1847, the Greek Revival style was popular in the Midwest, although it had reached its peak of popularity in the East during the 1830's. So, following the mode, Swartout achieved a dwelling that had the appearance of a Greek temple; an abode somewhat resembling a miniature Parthenon. The façade of this house, with its four fluted Doric columns, is typical of Greek classic architecture at its purest.

Here John Swartout and his family lived during the late 1840's and the ominous 1850's. Here he saw Little Fort grow in population and become an outlet for the furs, hides, pork, wheat, and lumber of the hinterland. And it was while living in this house that he was elected a trustee of the village in 1850, the community having been incorporated a year earlier and given the new name of "Waukegan." This was an Indian word meaning "fort" or "trading post." The village became a city in 1859.

When Lincoln Visited Evanston

SEVERAL YEARS ago, in an issue of the *Journal of the Illinois State Historical Society* (Vol. 35), the late Dr. James Taft Hatfield, then a retired Northwestern University professor, told of an unusual situation existing for almost a quarter of a century in Evanston. This had to do with the claims of at least half a dozen residents who, at various times, said that Abraham Lincoln stopped at their houses when he visited Evanston in 1860. All of these claims have been discounted, said Dr. Hatfield, with the exception of one, and it was in this house, and this one only, that Lincoln spent a night just six weeks before he was nominated for President of the United States.

Although somewhat altered, the house in which the memorable visit was made still stands. It has been moved twice and is now located at 2009 Dodge Avenue. For proof of the fact that Lincoln was a guest in this dwelling, Dr. Hatfield cited a historian, J. Seymour Currey, who was at one time president of the Evanston Historical Society. In addition to writing numerous other works, Currey, in 1914, penned a pamphlet titled "Abraham Lincoln's Visit to Evanston in 1860." It is in this pamphlet that we are given incontrovertible proof that the Civil War President stopped in the dwelling which now stands on Dodge Avenue.

But this is not its original site. From research by Dr. Hatfield, who took up the story of the house after Currey had written his pamphlet in 1914, we learn that it has been standing at its present location only since 1926. It had previously occupied another site after being moved from the spot at the northwest corner of Ridge Avenue and Church Street on which it stood when Lincoln was sheltered under its roof. This neighborhood has always been known to Evanstonians as "The Ridge." Today, on its Dodge Avenue site, the "Lincoln House" (as it is sometimes called) stands in the midst of the Negro section of Evanston, and, as Dr. Hatfield said, is "rather appropriately" occupied by Negro tenants.

At the time Lincoln was an overnight guest in this abode, it was occupied by Julius White, a friend of Lincoln's who was then harbor master of Chicago and a member of the Board of Trade. When Lincoln became President, he appointed White collector of the port of Chicago. But White soon resigned this office to raise a regiment, the 37th Illinois Volunteers. After the war, General White returned to Evanston and there he died in 1890. On exhibit in the Evanston Historical Society are two Army commissions to White signed by President Lincoln.

It was at the time Lincoln was an attorney in the "Sand Bar" case

James Taft Hatfield

Julius White House, Evanston, Built 1850's.

in Chicago that he came to General White's home in Evanston. He was then being talked of as a presidential possibility. He was escorted to Evanston in a Chicago & North Western Railway train by Harvey B. Hurd, neighbor of General White's and a founder and first president of the Evanston Historical Society. The day was April 5, 1860. Lincoln and Hurd sat near the stove in the railway coach and swapped stories.

    Upon arriving in Evanston, the future President was taken for a buggy ride about the village by his host, Julius White. The village then numbered about 1,200 residents and only five years earlier Northwestern University had erected its first building. When Lincoln was installed in the White home on "The Ridge," a crowd gathered in front and "serenaded" him. Lincoln came out on the veranda and delivered a brief address. Later that evening one of the guests, J. D. Ludlam, sang a few songs, with Miss Isabel Stewart at the piano. It was the first time they had seen each other. They were married a year later.

At that time the White home was a plain, two-story frame dwelling set back on a wide lawn and surrounded by a white picket fence. It was originally built by Alexander McDaniel and afterward sold to the Rev. Philo Judson. General White moved into it when he first came to Evanston in 1859.

"About 1884," wrote Dr. Hatfield, "General White's residence was moved eight blocks to a site at 1227 Elmwood Avenue, immediately south of the old Township High School, in a different quarter of the city, and was acquired by A. D. Sanders, who remodeled it to conform to more modern requirements. He added a third story, built a projecting gabled front-wing, a verandah and a bay window." But the bedroom which Lincoln occupied is still intact, said Dr. Hatfield. It is on the second floor, in the northwest corner of the house.

After Lincoln was elected President and the Civil War began, the young Evanstonian who sang for him in the White home, J. D. Ludlam, joined the Army and became an officer in the 8th Illinois Cavalry. His unit was sent to a camp near Washington, D. C. One day, while visiting the camp, President Lincoln recognized the tall, young Evanstonian. The Chief Executive remembered Ludlam's singing, and Miss Stewart's accompaniment on the piano, in the Evanston home of Julius White. The result of the encounter was that President Lincoln invited Ludlam to the White House to sing for him and Mrs. Lincoln.

It is recorded that Ludlam, who afterward became a major in the Union Army, sang the same "homely songs" on the occasion of the White House visit that he sang for Lincoln in the house on "The Ridge" in Evanston. What these songs were, however, is still unrecorded. "This echo of the Lincoln visit to Evanston," wrote J. Seymour Currey, "and the romance that had its beginning at that time, throws a golden haze of sentiment over the event we have been describing and heightens the interest that the episode otherwise possesses for all who take a pride in our Evanston annals."

"Rest Cottage"

NOT FAR from the Evanston campus of Northwestern University there stands a quaint old cottage, with scrollwork trim and board-and-batten siding. Although the cottage is of local interest because of its association with the university, it has wider renown as the home of an American woman who attracted international attention during the last decades of the nineteenth century. She was Frances E. Willard, temperance crusader, feminist, writer, orator, and a leader of numerous reform movements.

In 1865, the year that saw the end of the Civil War and the assassination of President Lincoln, Frances Willard's father built the board-and-batten cottage that has become one of Evanston's principal sights. At that time Miss Willard was twenty-six years old. She was already familiar with Evanston, having been graduated, six years earlier, from North Western Female College, which afterward was absorbed by Northwestern University. In addition to her father and mother, Miss Willard shared the newly-built Evanston cottage with her brother.

At the time her family dwelling was built, however, Miss Willard was unknown to fame, although only the year before she had published her first book, *Nineteen Beautiful Years*. This told of the life of her younger sister, Mary, who had died earlier and to whom Miss Willard had been devoted.

The two had come to Evanston in 1858 to attend North Western Female College. Some time afterward they had persuaded their father and mother, sturdy and devout Vermonters who had taken up life on a farm in Wisconsin, to join them and settle in Evanston.

After receiving her diploma from North Western Female College, Miss Willard continued her studies and became a teacher in a country school near Evanston. Afterward, she taught elsewhere and then went abroad, where she attended the University of Paris and traveled on the Continent.

Meanwhile, she began writing for weekly newspapers and magazines. Upon her return to the United States she joined the temperance crusade of 1874 and this marked the beginning of her career as a reform crusader.

During the remainder of her eventful and active life, the Willard family dwelling, which stands at 1728 Chicago Avenue, was her home. She called it "Rest Cottage" and thus it is known today, although her father, after he built it "on some new lots reclaimed from the swamp," called it "Rose Cottage" because of the rose bushes planted around it by the family.

Also planted here, in the yard at the rear, and by Miss Willard herself, were two chestnut trees. These are now full grown and shade the cottage in summer.

After serving as president of the Evanston College for Ladies in the early 1870's, Miss Willard was named first dean of the Woman's College

Frances E. Willard House, Evanston, Built 1865.

of Northwestern University when that institution became coeducational. Later, she founded the World's Woman's Christian Temperance Union, said to be the first international organization of women.

Work in this organization took her to all parts of the United States and Europe. As a temperance crusader she won the approval and friendship of a leading Englishwoman, Lady Henry Somerset, and even Queen Victoria is said to have shown an interest in the work of Frances Willard.

The international scope of Miss Willard's career, the brilliance and versatility of her mind, the honors bestowed on her, are all vividly illustrated by the Willard relics, mementos, and souvenirs now on display in Rest Cottage.

The cottage and its furnishings remain as they were before Miss Willard's death on February 18, 1898. Owned and maintained as a shrine by the W. C. T. U., the national headquarters of which occupy a modern two-story building at the rear of the dwelling, Rest Cottage attracted visitors from all parts of the United States and Europe during the one hundredth anniversary, in 1939, of Miss Willard's birth.

Of greatest interest among visitors to Rest Cottage is the room on the southwest corner of the second floor that Miss Willard called her den. A combined workshop, study, and library, it was here she did her writing and planned the activities that made her one of America's great women.

Her personally-annotated books, favorite Bible, writing materials, furniture, pictures, gifts, and many of her other cherished belongings are all in the den, just as they were when Miss Willard was at the height of her career. This room is warmed by a brick fireplace on which is inscribed Miss Willard's favorite motto: "Let Something Good Be Said."

This room contains the flat-topped oak desk where she wrote her famous "Polyglot Petition." It was a temperance petition addressed to the governments of the world and signed by more than seven million persons in fifty dialects. The sheets of the petition were mounted on rolls by Mrs. Rebecca C. Shuman of Evanston, and these rolls, if placed end to end, would extend five miles. This petition is now one of the prized exhibits in Rest Cottage.

Other exhibits in the den are Miss Willard's favorite rocker, in which she sat while writing her autobiography, *Glimpses of Fifty Years*, and while writing a book about Evanston called *A Classic Town;* her "Old Faithful" traveling bag; a tall grandfather's clock made by an ancestor, Simon Willard, famous Colonial clockmaker; and a large, handsomely-bound volume containing the originals of letters sent to her by many famous persons on the occasion of her visit to England in 1893.

In rooms on the main floor of the little cottage, rooms furnished in a manner typical of the 1880's and '90's, are several hundred other exhibits. The custodian of the cottage will show you Miss Willard's parlor organ, an embroidered "sampler" she made at the age of fourteen, a bicycle she learned to ride when she was fifty-three, a music box which plays "Home, Sweet Home" and other songs favored by Miss Willard, chinaware, glassware, and an old-fashioned English tea basket.

In a parlor on the north side of the cottage Miss Willard's longtime secretary and friend, Anna Gordon, maintained an office. This room is now the Anna Gordon memorial room. Miss Gordon, who in 1898 wrote *The Beautiful Life of Frances E. Willard*, continued to live in the cottage after Miss Willard's death, remaining here until her own death in 1931.

Northwest Territory Museum

ALTHOUGH not so old as most of the Illinois houses discussed in this book, the Dawes residence, at 225 Greenwood Avenue, in Evanston, is nonetheless an important landmark. For not only is it the home of a former Vice-President of the United States who was an international figure in the years after World War I, but it has been dedicated to perpetual use as a museum of the old Northwest Territory—the territory out of which the states of Illinois, Ohio, Indiana, Wisconsin, Michigan, and part of Minnesota were formed.

Designed in French Gothic style, this spacious brick mansion, under its stately old trees, has been the home of General Charles Gates Dawes for more than a third of a century. It is located just half a mile south of the tree-shaded campus of Northwestern University, and from its east windows the Dawes family can view the broad blue expanse of Lake Michigan. From the south veranda of this mansion General Dawes delivered the speech in 1924 in which he accepted the Republican nomina-

Chicago Daily News

Charles G. Dawes House, Evanston, Built 1894.

145

tion for Vice-President of the United States as the running mate of Calvin Coolidge.

But General Dawes was not the builder of this mansion. That honor fell to the Rev. Robert D. Sheppard, a professor at Northwestern University who, during the 1890's, served as the university's treasurer and business agent. Before going to Evanston, the Rev. Mr. Sheppard was a minister in Chicago. He was born in Chicago in 1846, the son of a pioneer lumber merchant and early school teacher of the city. It was in 1894 that Dr. Sheppard built the residence in Evanston and General Dawes acquired it in 1909.

At the time he moved into this house, General Dawes was forging ahead in business and politics. He had already served as comptroller of the currency in the administration of President McKinley and, afterward, he established the Central Republic Bank of Chicago. Before going to Chicago, he practiced law in Lincoln, Nebraska, and while there met, and formed a lifelong friendship with Lieutenant John J. Pershing, who was to become commander of American forces in World War I.

General Dawes was born at Marietta, Ohio, on August 27, 1865. His great-great-grandfather was Manasseh Cutler, who was a partner of General Rufus Putnam in the establishment of the Ohio Company, the organization which settled the Northwest Territory. Acting for the Ohio Company, composed largely of officers of the Revolutionary War, Manasseh Cutler negotiated the purchase from the Continental Congress of 1,500,000 acres of land, on which Marietta, Ohio, was founded on May 7, 1788.

With Manasseh Cutler as an ancestor, it was but natural for General Dawes to become interested in the history of the Northwest Territory early in his career. During the eventful years following, he continued to pursue his hobby of collecting material on this subject; material which he stored in his Evanston home. Here, too, he wrote numerous books and, as a pianist, composed the famous "Melody in A Major." His interest in the Northwest Territory was shared by his wife, whose great-grandfather, Paul Fearing, was the first lawyer west of the Allegheny Mountains and who was the first delegate of the Northwest Territory to the Continental Congress.

Rich in historical papers and documents, as well as pioneer furniture and exhibits connected with the career of General Dawes, the Greenwood Avenue residence has been given to Northwestern University and will become the Northwestern Historical Center. It will also shelter the Evanston Historical Society. General Dawes and his wife will continue to live in the mansion during their lifetimes.

"Craigie Lea"

AMONG old mansions in the extreme northeast corner of the state, one of the most venerable and best-known is the MacLeish home at Glencoe. The mansion is nearly hidden from view in a grove of white oaks and pines and its landscaped grounds front on an expanse of Lake Michigan. It is a dwelling that dates almost from the beginning of North Shore settlement.

Of greater interest, however, is the fact that it is the country seat of three generations of a family that has played—and is still playing— an important role in the literary and artistic, as well as the commercial and educational development of Illinois. It is of interest, too, for its architecture, representing as it does a style much in vogue during the grandiose days of the late Victorian era.

It was here that Archibald MacLeish, nationally known poet and former librarian of the Library of Congress, was born and reared, as was his brother, Norman H., a well-known Illinois artist. A generation ago the father and mother of these two brothers, Mr. and Mrs. Andrew MacLeish, were leaders in business, cultural, and religious activities of Chicago and the state at large.

Named in honor of the memory of a deceased member of this family, who also was reared in the Glencoe home, is a fast, modern destroyer of the United States Navy, the *U. S. S. MacLeish*, which was on patrol duty in the Atlantic during World War II. It was named after another son of the MacLeishes, Kenneth, who, as a lieutenant in the United States naval aviation forces, was killed in action during World War I. An officer on this destroyer during the later conflict was young Hugh MacLeish, kin of the man after whom the vessel is named.

An attractive, privately-printed little volume, *Life of Andrew MacLeish*, tells that the house in Glencoe was completed in 1891. It was named "Craigie Lea" after Mr. MacLeish's favorite Scottish song, "Thou Bonnie Wood of Craigie Lea," by Robert Tannahill. In his book the elder MacLeish wrote: "In 1889 we secured beautiful property fronting on the lake at Glencoe, Illinois, and, after a few years of summer residence upon it, finally decided to make it our permanent home. We have never regretted this step."

At the time he built his suburban residence Andrew MacLeish was widely known as a successful Chicago merchant and one of the prominent figures of State Street. This position he was to maintain for the rest of his long and useful life. As a member of a pioneer wholesale dry goods

firm founded by Samuel Carson and John T. Pirie, it was Andrew Mac-
Leish who, in 1867, established that firm's retail department store, now
known as Carson Pirie Scott & Co. He remained its head until his
death in 1928 at the age of eighty-nine.

A native of Scotland, Andrew MacLeish came to Chicago in 1856
and worked as a clerk in a dry goods store on Lake Street, then the main
shopping street of the town. Later he set up a store of his own at Kewanee. His health failing, he went to live on a farm near Golconda,
Illinois. When his health was restored he taught school at Golconda.
Then, in 1859, he returned to Chicago and once more entered the dry
goods business.

After Craigie Lea was completed Andrew MacLeish brought with
him into the new dwelling his son by a previous marriage, Bruce, whose
mother had died a year after his birth. This son, upon reaching maturity, joined his father's firm and today, as vice-president of Carson
Pirie Scott & Co., occupies almost as high a position in the mercantile
world as had his father.

Well known as a merchant when Craigie Lea was erected, Andrew
MacLeish was equally well known as a leader in education and as
one of the founders of the University of Chicago. His wife also occupied a high position in the educational world. Before her marriage
to the State Street merchant Martha Hilliard had served as president
of Rockford College. Both she and her husband were early advocates
of the progressive movement in education fostered by John Dewey, and
Dewey was a frequent visitor at Craigie Lea.

Others who came to Craigie Lea in its early years were Dr. William
Rainey Harper, Thomas W. Goodspeed, and Colonel Francis Parker, all
noted educators; well-known social workers like Jane Addams, Mary
McDowell, Ellen Gates, and Julia Lathrop; and on one occasion there
came Sir George Adam Smith, one of the foremost of Scottish scholars
and divines. In recent years, Craigie Lea has welcomed many writers
and artists, including Carl Sandburg, Margaret Bourke-White, Eunice
Tietjens, Lorado Taft, Francis Chapin, Aaron Bohrod, and Gertrude
Abercrombie.

The original MacLeish estate consisted of seventeen acres and
cost $10,000. The house, a great three-story residence of brick and
frame construction with conical towers, dormers, high-pitched gables,
and other characteristics of the French chateau style popular in the
1890's, cost $25,000 to build and was designed by William Carbys
Zimmerman and John F. Flanders, two well-known Chicago architects.
The estate today consists of ten acres.

Chicago Daily News

Andrew MacLeish House, Glencoe, Built 1891.

The interior of the house, with more than thirty large, well-lighted rooms, is tastefully furnished and reflects the personalities of quiet, cultivated people who place high value on artistic and intellectual pursuits. Paneled in golden oak, cherry wood, and mahogany, and warmed by hospitable fireplaces of ornamental tile, the rooms contain shelves of books, portraits in oil of the elder MacLeishes, many paintings of the Illinois countryside by Norman MacLeish, a handsome grand piano, antique furniture, sculptural pieces, and various family heirlooms.

During the many years she reigned as chatelaine of Craigie Lea, the late Mrs. MacLeish engaged in religious and cultural activities that made her one of the most esteemed women of Chicago and the North Shore. She was at one time president of the Chicago Woman's Club. It was through her efforts that the Women's American Foreign Mission Baptist Society was formed. And each year, on the lawn of Craigie Lea, she presided at a garden fete that was one of the outstanding annual events of social life on the North Shore.

Underground Station

JUST BEFORE entering the leafy streets of Princeton, ancient seat of early Illinois abolitionism, motorists on U. S. Highway 6 (old Peru road) notice, on the right, a trim old-fashioned white farmhouse with a sign on its comfortable veranda reading: "Owen Lovejoy Homestead—Underground Station." That house is one of the oldest in Bureau County and ranks among the most important of the historic sights in that section of the Illinois River country.

Here lived, during most of his career, Owen Lovejoy, preacher-statesman of Illinois, leader of the antislavery movement in the state before the Civil War, and younger brother of the Alton editor, Elijah Parish Lovejoy, whose writings against slavery brought about his assassination by a proslavery mob. The Lovejoy brothers occupy a secure place in American history as fearless champions of human freedom, of racial equality, and of the rights of free speech and free press.

Somewhat obscured by the fame of his slain brother, Owen Lovejoy was just as fiery and influential an abolitionist as was Elijah. Throughout the fifty-three years of his life he devoted himself unflinchingly to the antislavery cause. He lived long enough to see his friend, President Abraham Lincoln, free the slaves, and, a year before his death in 1864, he heard, as a congressman from Illinois, the reading of the Emancipation Proclamation.

The story of the house in which he lived goes back to the year 1843 when he married the woman who occupied it. She was Mrs. Eunice S. Denham, whose late husband, Butler Denham, had been an early settler of Bureau County. He is recorded as one of the group of twenty residents of Princeton Township who, in 1838, voted for incorporation of the village of Princeton. Another in the group was John H. Bryant, brother of the poet, William Cullen Bryant.

A native of Albion, Maine, where he was born January 6, 1811, and where his father was a clergyman, Owen Lovejoy, after attending Bowdoin College, came west to Alton in 1836 and entered the ministry. He soon joined his older brother in the fight against slavery. Alton was then a hotbed of pro- and antislavery factions. In time, several of Elijah Lovejoy's printing presses were destroyed or thrown into the river by proslavery elements.

On November 7, 1837, a new press arrived at Alton, consigned to Elijah Lovejoy. It was placed in a warehouse for safekeeping. The warehouse was owned by Captain Benjamin Godfrey, whose home at

150

Godfrey, Illinois, is now a residential landmark of the state. Hearing of the new press, a down-river mob descended on the Godfrey warehouse, set it on fire, and shot and killed Elijah Lovejoy when he attempted to protect the press. Kneeling beside the body of his slain brother, Owen Lovejoy vowed "never to forsake the cause that had been sprinkled with his brother's blood."

During the seventeen years that Owen Lovejoy served as minister in Princeton, he never forgot that vow. Always he preached against

Owen Lovejoy House, Princeton, Built 1830's.

slavery, even though Princeton contained some proslavery elements. His home on the edge of town became a station of the Underground Railway—a system by which abolitionists passed escaped slaves secretly from house to house until they reached Canada and freedom. In the official guidebook to Princeton, written by George V. Martin, author of a recent novel, *For Our Vines Have Tender Grapes*, an incident is given of Owen Lovejoy's abolitionist activities.

"One day an escaped Negro," says the guidebook, "was captured and chained to a tree just outside of the county courthouse. Lovejoy awaited his chance, and when no one was in the immediate vicinity, he told the Negro how he might escape, and the hour when it would be most nearly possible. In some manner unexplained in the history of the case, the Negro slipped out of his bonds and made a mad dash for the Lovejoy home at the appointed hour.

"A mob immediately followed, demanded the return of the former slave, and threatened violence. Lovejoy held them at bay with a rifle, promising death to the first to enter the yard. No man entered. That night the Negro was dressed in women's clothes, given a horse, and directed to the next station of the Underground Railway. Scores of others were assisted to escape by Lovejoy, but in less spectacular manner."

When he was elected to the state legislature in 1854 on the ticket of the newly-founded Republican Party, Owen Lovejoy continued his fight against slavery. Then, upon being elected to Congress in 1856, he became a national leader of the abolitionist movement. "To him," says an authoritative work, "fell the honor of proposing the bill by which slavery in all the territories of the United States was abolished forever."

Following Owen Lovejoy's death while on a visit to Brooklyn in 1864, President Lincoln wrote of him: "My personal acquaintance with him . . . has been one of increasing respect and esteem, ending, with his life, in no less than affection on my part. . . . To the day of his death, it would scarcely wrong any other to say he was my most generous friend."

Following the death of her husband, Mrs. Lovejoy and her children continued to live in the old Princeton farmhouse. She died at an advanced age. Six Lovejoy children were born and reared here—Sarah, who became the wife of William R. French, Chicago; Owen G., who was an attorney in Princeton; Ida, who was at one time Princeton's postmistress; Sophia, who married Charles Dickinson, Chicago; Elijah Parish, who became a Bureau County farmer; and Charles P., who was a leading veterinary surgeon of Princeton.

Standing in a grove of maples beside the highway, the ancient house is remarkably well preserved. It is a low, two-story, frame dwelling with a wide porch along its front. Having recognized the historical value of the house, its onetime owner, the late J. L. Spaulding, who was then the oldest practicing attorney of Bureau County, converted it into a period museum. He was assisted in this work by his daughter, Mrs. Sue Gross, an antique collector.

In each room of the house may be seen, simply and comfortably arranged, articles of furniture dating from pre-Civil War days. Here are walnut tables, chairs, and chests, trundle beds, spinning wheels, pewter ware, and four-poster beds. On the walls hang old-fashioned family portraits as well as original paintings by an Illinois artist, Mary Skinner. And over the fireplace is a bronze tablet containing an eloquent tribute to Owen Lovejoy as an outstanding American.

Home of a Poet's Brother

AMONG long-settled families at Princeton, seat of Bureau County and hub of a thriving farm area, one of the best known is the Bryant family. Descendants of this family, which was established in Illinois more than a century ago by four brothers of the poet, William Cullen Bryant, now live on prosperous farms in Bureau County and adjacent territory. And they occupy comfortable, well-preserved old family seats which are landmarks of that part of the state.

Of the four Bryant brothers who came to Illinois between the years 1830 and 1833, the one who attained most prominence in the state was John Howard Bryant. Because of the important role he played in the early development of Illinois, and because of his associations with some of the state's historic personages, his house in Princeton is of interest to students of history. Of interest, too, is the dwelling of his brother, Cyrus, which stands but a few blocks from John's house. Cyrus was also a figure of importance in pioneer days.

Of John H. Bryant, a standard biographical reference work says: "Like his friend Lincoln he was large, powerful, and of great endurance, able in the course of a day to split a hundred rails, labor sixteen hours

John H. Bryant House, Princeton, Built 1840's.

153

about the farm, or ride seventy-five miles across country on horseback. In temper and interests he was of much the same stuff as his brother, William Cullen, to whom he was devoted. Although farming was his chief occupation, he built roads and bridges, manufactured brick for a time, and edited a local newspaper. He was probably the most useful citizen in his community."

John Bryant and his brother, Cyrus, came to Princeton in 1832 and built log cabins. Having prospered with their farming, the two built brick houses in the early 1840's and these are the dwellings which survive. The address of the Cyrus Bryant house in 1110 South Main Street, and that of the John Bryant abode is 1518 South Main Street. It is understood that the Cyrus Bryant dwelling was designed by Alvah Whitmarsh, pioneer carpenter-architect of Princeton and grandfather of Herma Clark (see the next chapter).

A guest in these two houses on several occasions was William Cullen Bryant and these visits to Illinois inspired the poet to write "The Prairies." Although it is not recorded that he ever visited either of the Bryant homes, Abraham Lincoln is said to have delivered an address at a Fourth of July gathering in Bryant's Woods in 1856. In these years John Bryant was an antislavery advocate and his big brick house was a station of the Underground Railroad—as was the Owen Lovejoy abode.

In the *Princeton Guide*, we learn that John Bryant "was a member of the state legislature from Bureau, Peoria, and Stark in 1842, and again in 1858. . . . In 1848 he was one of the early editors of the first newspaper to be established in Bureau County; in 1860 was a delegate to the convention in Chicago which nominated Abraham Lincoln; was appointed collector of internal revenue by President Lincoln in 1862."

Not to be overlooked is the fact that John Bryant, too, was a poet. His books, *Poems* and *Life and Poems*, were published in 1855 and 1894 respectively. His brother, Cyrus, was one of the founders of Bureau County and its first county clerk. Another brother, Arthur, founded a nursery in 1845 which is still in existence. And a third brother, Colonel Austin Bryant, played a creditable part in the development of the county.

On the lawn adjacent to the Cyrus Bryant house rests a boulder with a tablet on it containing the words: "To commemorate the one hundredth anniversary of the coming of the brothers Cyrus P. and John Howard Bryant to Putnam, now Bureau County, Illinois, and pre-empting this land. In this grove—an early landmark known as Round Point—they built their log cabin, beginning the settlement which later developed into the city of Princeton."

"Keepsake Cottage"

AFTER she became widely known for her entertainingly nostalgic "When Chicago Was Young" column in *The Chicago Sunday Tribune* and as an author, playwright, and monologist, Herma Clark returned to her native town of Princeton and acquired a century-old house that now is as much a landmark as are the Owen Lovejoy and John Bryant houses. Here, amid the collection of relics, souvenirs, and antiques that has evoked the name "Keepsake Cottage" for her house, Herma Clark continues to write her column and books like *The Elegant Eighties*, and to add to her repertoire of monologues, such as her "Bustles and Bangs," "Albums and Antimacassars," and "Farm and Fireside," which are as popular as her newspaper column.

In her role as a platform speaker specializing in modes and manners of the Elegant Eighties and Neighborly Nineties, often wearing elaborate costumes of those gaudy periods, Herma Clark is frequently absent from Keepsake Cottage, delighting audiences in towns and cities of the Midwest. She also is in Chicago at weekly intervals, attending to her newspaper work and engaging in various club and social activities. When not thus involved, however, the gracious, whimsical author of the "Martha Esmond" letters may be found in her northern Illinois home, entertaining old friends and welcoming new ones. Living with Miss Clark in Keepsake Cottage is her sister, Mrs. H. A. Gossard, who, besides being joint owner of the house, serves as its mistress during Miss Clark's absences.

Like most of the other houses in Princeton, Keepsake Cottage is white-painted, kept in trim condition, and surrounded by a spacious lawn. On one side of the house may be seen hollyhocks, descendants of some from the garden of the humorous poet, Bert Leston Taylor.

Evidence that this cottage is almost a century old, although its comfortable porch is of more recent date, is provided in the returns on its façade, these being in the mode of the Greek Revival. It is believed that the builder of the Clark cottage was John Crittenden, a pioneer settler of Princeton, and that he erected it about 1850. Another Princeton pioneer and a neighbor of Crittenden's was Alvah Whitmarsh, grandfather of Herma Clark. As an early carpenter-architect, Alvah Whitmarsh designed and built many houses which are still standing in the town.

A native of Princeton, where her parents, Major and Mrs. Atherton Clark, were highly esteemed residents, Miss Clark, after completing her studies at Oberlin College, went to Chicago and there met the person who, she says, had the greatest influence on her life—the Chicago society leader, Mrs. William Blair. "As a young woman," writes Herma Clark in *The Elegant Eighties*, "hardly out of teen-age, intent on seeking fame and fortune in the nearest large city, I left the Illinois town in which I had grown up. A kind fate sent me the opportunity to act as secretary to Mr. William Blair, retired businessman, who had been the first wholesale hardware dealer in the infant Chicago.

"On his death, I remained with his widow, as her secretary. . . . Mrs. Blair was a beautiful woman, and as she drove down Michigan Avenue in her *vis-a-vis*, . . . she was a type of great lady indeed. But it was not only her outward appearance, it was her inward and spiritual grace, which so deeply impressed me. It is not too much to say that, aside from my own family, she was the person who most influenced me."

When Herma Clark acquired the old Crittenden house in 1947, she found it was in need of repairs and improvements. In characteristic fashion, she became so enthusiastic over the work of restoration that she infected her relatives and some of her close friends and they volunteered to help her. Writing in her delightful *Guide Book to Keepsake Cottage*, Miss Clark says: "It may be asked if the matter of getting relatives and friends thus to labor presented no difficulties. Our answer is: 'None whatever.' It was done by a sublimation of the principle employed by Tom Sawyer, when he got his fence whitewashed. Tom made it hard to get a chance to use the whitewash brush on that Missouri back fence. Our method was to mention our intention to write the story of the renovation of the house and to ask, 'Wouldn't you like to be in the book?' So here is the promised volume."

Today, the interior of Keepsake Cottage is a veritable museum of the Elegant Eighties. But in it there is none of the stuffiness, the overcrowding, of an 1880 interior. After passing through the small entrance hall—which contains, among other things, an old hatrack and an oval-framed picture of Herma Clark's father in his Civil War officer's uniform —and through a doorway above which hangs a cross-stitched motto: "God Bless Our Home," the visitor finds himself in the living room. Here are numerous articles from the home of the late Mrs. Blair, among them a long gold-framed mirror, walnut and oak chairs, a teakwood table, and a bronze lamp base, which was originally a Japanese vase purchased at the 1893 fair in Chicago.

Other objects of interest in the living room are wax flowers under a glass dome, several oils by the late Princeton artist, Edith Taber, a painting by Mrs. Grace Hall Hemingway, mother of the novelist, and a por-

Herma Clark House, Princeton, Built 1850.

trait of Herma Clark by the London artist, Dorothy Vicaji, who also painted Queen Alexandra. From the living room the visitor passes into the dining room, and here the most valued piece of furniture is a round table with a cherry wood top, which was made by Grandfather Whitmarsh. Among the books on shelves in the dining room are two old volumes—*Literary Remains of Willis Gaylord Clark*, written by a granduncle of Miss Clark's, and *History of the Ninth Illinois Cavalry*, a regiment in which Miss Clark's father served during the Civil War. In other rooms of the cottage, especially in Miss Clark's study, are found a great variety of quaint, sometimes amusing, heirlooms, mementos, and keepsakes, either from friends of the author or from relatives.

Upon leaving Keepsake Cottage, nestling under its shade trees, the visitor is likely to hear the bell in the Congregational Church tower near by ringing out the hour or half-hour—a bell which owes its existence to Princeton's most famous historical personage, the Rev. Owen Lovejoy.

Home of an Abolitionist Leader

ONE of the famous abolitionists in northern Illinois was John Hossack, who used his house in Ottawa as a station of the Underground Railway. Because of this, the Hossack house has become a historic landmark and shares interest among sight-seers with several other historic dwellings in Ottawa, notably the homes of General W. H. L. Wallace, and State Senator William Reddick.

But the Hossack house is of interest for other reasons than its association with the abolitionist cause. Not only was the owner of the residence a leader in the antislavery movement but he was an influential grain dealer of the Illinois River Valley and the maternal grandfather of three men who became well-known Chicago merchants. The house, too, appeals to architectural students, since it is an example of the Southern Colonial style of domestic building, one of the several styles which prevailed in Illinois during the 1840's and '50's.

According to data compiled by the Historic American Buildings Survey, John Hossack built his residence in 1854 and 1855. The architect was Sylvannus Grow, of Chicago, and the builder was Alonzo Edwards. The present address of the house is 210 West Prospect Avenue. Here John Hossack lived as an influential citizen of the Illinois River city and here he reared his family.

"The memory of Hossack," writes C. C. Tisler in his interesting booklet, *Lincoln's in Town*, which deals with Lincoln's visits to Ottawa, "lives on in the hearts of those who love freedom, who hate tyranny and who have the courage to defy the law if they consider it unjust, rather than submit supinely. His courage led him to defy the Fugitive Slave Law in 1859 by aiding escaped Negro slaves, so that he was jailed and fined in Federal Court in Chicago, in 1860, along with other Ottawans. The confinement was nominal. City officials took them riding and gave a banquet for them. The jailing of men and women for defying the Fugitive Slave Law was not popular in the North in 1859 and 1860."

There is a story current in Ottawa that Abraham Lincoln was a visitor in the Hossack house but Lincoln scholars have not been able to prove this. It is certain, however, that John Hossack was present on that August day in 1858 when Lincoln and Stephen A. Douglas staged the first of their historic joint debates in Ottawa. During the Civil War, one of John Hossack's sons, Henry Lens Hossack, headed a company of soldiers he raised himself and, after the war, was active in Grand Army of the Republic affairs. He was also a leading Ottawa merchant.

158

Historic American Buildings Survey

John Hossack House, Ottawa, Built 1854.

After the death of John Hossack, the house on Prospect Avenue was occupied by his son-in-law and daughter, Mr. and Mrs. John Edwin Scott. During this time, John Edwin Scott conducted a dry goods store in Ottawa. He later moved up to Chicago and became the first partner of Samuel Carson and John T. Pirie in the ownership of a dry goods store, well known today as Carson Pirie Scott & Co. Two of John Scott's sons, Robert L. and Frederick H., are members of the department store firm.

The old Hossack house, with its typical two-story Southern-style gallery and its spacious mid-Victorian rooms, is now the home of Mr. and Mrs. Thomas R. Godfrey. He is a well-known Ottawa real-estate man. White painted, well preserved, and surrounded by attractive shrubbery, it is easily distinguishable as one of the city's landmarks.

On the North Bluff

ALTHOUGH a monument in honor of General W. H. L. Wallace, one of Illinois' great Civil War commanders, stands in Tennessee on the spot where he fell mortally wounded during the Battle of Shiloh, his memory is much more effectively recalled by a landmark in the northern part of the state of his adoption. This is the general's home, a spacious stone residence on a bluff north of Ottawa. It is now a historic shrine, owned and maintained by the state, and annually visited by hundreds of sightseers and students of the Civil War.

The Wallace home has of late attracted the attention of architectural historians as well as specialists in the field of pioneer American interior design. Its stone exterior contains evidences of Gothic ornamentation, a style which was beginning to appear in America in the late 1850's, and its interior, with its original Wallace furnishings and bric-a-brac, is representative of the homes of the upper class during the Civil War period.

This dwelling is of interest, too, to Lincoln scholars. General Wallace, who also was a lawyer, was one of Lincoln's friends and strong supporters. Among exhibits in this house are the bed in which Lincoln is said to have slept, the checkerboard on which he played, and his favorite chair. These, possibly, may have come from the near-by mansion of Judge T. Lyle Dickey, father-in-law of Wallace, who also was a close friend of Lincoln's but was his political antagonist. Lincoln is known to have visited the Dickeys at various times—conceivably he took much interest in the construction of the Wallace home which started in 1858 and continued for two years. Other exhibits in the Wallace house include a beautiful dress General Wallace gave his wife when Lincoln was elected President.

It was shortly before this incident that the stone house on the North Bluff was completed at a cost of $25,000. The house was supplied with fine walnut furniture and other household articles which Mrs. Wallace purchased in Boston. As it stood on an estate of four acres shaded by stately oaks, the Wallaces promptly called their place "The Oaks."

Although General Wallace attained his greatest fame in the Civil War, which opened only a year after his mansion on the Ottawa bluff was completed, it was not his first encounter with the grim ways of warfare. For he had earlier served in the Mexican War, taking part in the Battle of Buena Vista and several other engagements. There he became adjutant with a rank of second lieutenant. When the war ended he re-

160

turned to Illinois, once more took up the practice of law, and in 1852 was elected state's attorney.

A native of Urbana, Ohio, where he was born July 8, 1821, William Hervey Lamb Wallace was brought to Illinois by his parents when he was eleven years old. He received a common school education, studied

W. H. L. Wallace House, Ottawa, Built 1858.

law, and was admitted to practice in 1845. He made his way to Ottawa, then a lively river town, and here he married a daughter of T. Lyle Dickey, an attorney who became a justice of the State Supreme Court and, as a colonel in the Civil War, served as commander of cavalry on the staff of General Grant.

When the Civil War started and his friend President Lincoln issued a call for troops, William Wallace promptly enlisted and was appointed colonel of the 11th Illinois Regiment of volunteers. Into the conflict he carried with him a flag presented to the regiment by the ladies of Ottawa —and which now is on exhibition in this house. As commander of the 2d Division, Army of the Tennessee, Brigadier General Wallace was mortally wounded on April 6, 1862, at the Battle of Shiloh. He died at Savannah, Tennessee, on April 10, 1862.

The general is buried in the family cemetery on the grounds of his estate on the North Bluff. His widow and daughter, Isabel, continued to occupy The Oaks for many years after his death. Mrs. Wallace died in 1889. In 1909 the general's daughter completed and published a biographical volume, *Life and Letters of Gen. W. H. L. Wallace*. After Isabel Wallace's death in 1933, a movement to have the state purchase the house for a historic shrine was started by the late State Representative Edward G. Hayne, of Ottawa. He attained his objective in 1940.

The house is a square, two-story dwelling of rough-faced limestone. It contains twelve large rooms, eight of which have marble fireplaces. All rooms are outfitted with the original Wallace furnishings—elegant walnut tables, chairs, chests, beds, and a grand piano purchased in 1850. Side lights of colored glass at the front entrance depict scenes of Chicago as it appeared a hundred years ago.

In such surroundings, the visitor may view a large collection of relics, souvenirs, curios, and trophies associated with early Illinois history, the Mexican and Civil Wars, and with General Wallace, President Lincoln, General Grant, Colonel Dickey, and other figures of the state's and the country's past.

Library in a Mansion

NUMEROUS old mansions throughout Illinois have been converted into public libraries, and an interesting example of this is the venerable Reddick residence in Ottawa. For more than half a century it has served as a library and this fact has helped to make it one of the most familiar buildings of the Illinois River city. Its location, too, adds to its familiarity, for it is situated adjacent to Ottawa's principal recreation spot, Washington Park.

An imposing, old-style mansion, three stories high and redolent of the gaudy era of American architecture, this house, it is apparent at first glance, was built by some man of wealth and importance in Ottawa life. The man who built this house, which stands at the northwest corner of Columbus and Lafayette streets, was William Reddick. He constructed his home in 1859, at a cost of about $60,000. It is of red

William Reddick House, Ottawa, Built 1859.

163

brick, with white stone facing, and there is a legend that the bricks were hauled by wagons from Milwaukee. Reddick built on such a grand scale that his house and outbuildings occupied half the block bounded by Lafayette, Columbus, and Washington streets, with an alley at the west end of the property. The main building was his home. Along the alley were a horse barn, a carriage house, and a two-story smokehouse of such size that now it has been converted into the home of the library custodian.

After its completion the Reddick abode became one of the show places of Ottawa. Here, during the Civil War and in the years following, the Reddicks reigned as one of the first families of their city. Reddick was elected to the state senate for three successive terms beginning in 1846 and to a fourth term in 1870. He served his final two-year period at Springfield with distinction and, when it was over, returned to Ottawa and spent the remainder of his life there.

In his magnificent house overlooking the trees of Washington Park, William Reddick lived to a ripe age and here he died in 1885. When his will was opened it was found that he had set up an endowment fund of $100,000 for the founding and maintenance of a library in his home. The library was established here three years later. Since that time several generations of Ottawans have derived knowledge and pleasure from the great array of books lining the walls of the old Reddick mansion. Also in the library is Reddick's indenture paper by which he was bound out as an apprentice glass worker. His first $1,000 was accumulated by two years of work as a glass blower in Washington, D. C.— from 1832 to 1834.

In addition to the library Reddick's will left a hundred acres of land to La Salle County for "enlargement of the county home." That land, which is still owned by the public, is underlain with millions of tons of fine silica sand and is now worth many times as much as all his property at the time of his death.

Queen Anne Style Mansion

ON A SPRING DAY in 1833, shortly after the small log settlement of Chicago had been incorporated as a town, a lanky lad of twenty-one arrived there aboard a sailing vessel. His name was John Dean Caton. He had come to Chicago determined to practice law and equally determined never to have anything more to do with a farm. Only a short time earlier he had suffered a severe cut on his foot while working on a farm in his native state of New York.

In later life, however, when John Dean Caton was one of the best-known men in Illinois, being then an associate justice of the Illinois Supreme Court, he evidently broke his early resolve and acquired a large farm on a bluff above Ottawa. Here he erected a magnificent Queen Anne style mansion which became one of the noteworthy old residential landmarks of Illinois. In winter, when the trees surrounding it are bare, its red brick, castle-like bulk, with its gable roof, great round bays, dormers, spacious veranda, and tall chimneys, may be seen from the streets of the city below.

In addition to Justice Caton, this house is associated with numerous other prominent persons, among them the justice's son, Arthur J. Caton; Mrs. Marshall Field; Senator Albert J. Beveridge, and Mrs. Beveridge. In the early years of the present century it was a summer social center where house parties, lawn fetes, and outdoor sports events attracted the attention of society editors in all parts of the state.

Because of the charm of its location, above the rooftops of Ottawa and the sparkling expanse of the Illinois River, the Caton house brought other leading Illinoisans to this river bluff and in time a colony of country homes was established here.

So far as can be determined, Justice Caton erected his brick mansion early in the 1880's. He was then retired from public life. At that period Queen Anne architecture was in vogue among well-to-do citizens. And in this class of citizens was Judge Caton, for in 1867 he had enhanced his worldly fortune by selling his interest in a pioneer Illinois telegraph company to the then newly organized Western Union Telegraph Company.

He was not sitting on the Supreme Court bench at that time, having retired from office in 1864 after twenty-two years' service, mostly as chief justice, in the state's highest tribunal. While on the bench, he served with distinction, and his decisions are scattered through some twenty-seven volumes of Illinois reports.

165

It is known that Judge Caton first saw Ottawa when he attended a political convention there in 1834. The river town was, at the time of this visit, in a boom stage as a result of the opening of the Illinois and Michigan Canal, which ran through it. After his first appointment as associate justice of the Supreme Court in 1842—justices then traveled on circuits—John Caton again saw Ottawa.

"Judge Caton's circuit," says an old volume of Illinois biographies, "consisted of twelve counties, and at Ottawa, the county seat of one of them, he decided to make his home. Here, on one of the bluffs overlooking the rich valley of the Illinois, he built a comfortable mansion, surrounded by groves and lawns, and commanding a view of the most beautiful scenery in the state."

This mansion was his first home. Here was born, in 1851, the judge's son, Arthur, who was reared here until he was sixteen. This house was then replaced by the present brick dwelling. In his new abode Judge Caton lived the life of a country gentleman, tending to his blooded stock, studying nature, reading in his library, and engaging in literary and scientific pursuits which resulted in half-a-dozen noteworthy books from his pen. He also, in company with his wife, made occasional trips to Europe and the Far East.

At a house party in the Caton home young Arthur Caton met Miss Delia Spencer, attractive daughter of one of the founders of the Chicago hardware firm of Hibbard, Spencer, Bartlett & Co. They were afterward married and lived with the elder Catons at Ottawa. During the 1890's Arthur Caton was a leading Chicago lawyer, sportsman, and clubman. By then he and his father had established a Chicago residence on fashionable Calumet Avenue. Among their closest neighbors and friends there were the Marshall Fields.

Upon the death of Judge Caton in 1895 the Ottawa estate fell to Arthur Caton, and here he engaged in his favorite hobbies—raising thoroughbred horses and pedigreed dogs. His wife, meanwhile, won wide admiration as a hostess. After the death of Arthur Caton in 1904 the Ottawa mansion became the property of his widow. Some ten months later she was married to Marshall Field, who then was a widower and considered one of the richest men in the world. But this marriage was destined not to last long, for Marshall Field died of pneumonia five months later.

In the years following, Mrs. Marshall Field continued to occupy her Ottawa estate, spending the summer months here. In winter she lived either at her Chicago residence or at her imposing home in Washington, D. C. Often with her as companions in the Ottawa mansion were her

John D. Caton House,* Ottawa, Built in early 1880's.

niece, Mrs. Albert J. Beveridge, and the latter's husband, Senator Albert J. Beveridge, of Indiana. With the death of Mrs. Field in 1937 the Ottawa landmark fell to Mrs. Beveridge. She afterward sold it to Anthony S. ("Hum") Berry, a well-known Ottawa merchant and real-estate man.

Under the guidance of Mr. Berry, the old Caton home was made the nucleus of a suburban development on the North Bluff, known as Field Hill Estates. Many recently-built homes, white-painted and bright, surround the venerable Caton mansion under its elms and evergreens.

Some remodeling has been done in the interior of the mansion but on the whole it retains much of its onetime splendor. Here are twenty-eight great rooms trimmed in fine woods and adorned with marble and tile fireplaces, parquet floors, and highly ornamental built-in cabinets. Some of the rooms retain their original brass and copper chandeliers, one of which is handsomely embellished with opalescent and ruby glass.

* The house has been razed since this article was written.

Above the River

AFTER it was built almost three quarters of a century ago, the impressive Hegeler mansion, standing like a baronial castle on a bluff above the rooftops of La Salle, was an object of awe to the Illinois River steamboat men of the 1870's and 1880's.

Today, with its stone walls faded by age and its environs crowded by later houses, this mansion arouses the curiosity of a new generation of river men—the men who operate the modern, Diesel-engined towboats. What they observe is one of La Salle's outstanding residential landmarks, a landmark that once was known throughout the country as the seat of a new religious movement.

This tall, three-story stone dwelling, with its French-style mansard roof and mansarded cupola standing out against the sky, was built in 1874 by Edward C. Hegeler, who at that time was one of the leading industrialists of America and La Salle's most prominent citizen.

Thirteen years after the completion of his residence Hegeler established the Open Court Publishing Company for the dissemination of his scientific-religious beliefs. From the first floor of his La Salle mansion went out tracts, books, and magazines, including *The Monist*, to all parts of the country and even to foreign lands.

Before erecting his house, however, Hegeler had established himself as one of the builders of La Salle. This he did by founding, in association with another man, the Matthiessen & Hegeler Zinc Company, which in time became one of the largest zinc works in America and La Salle's principal industry. The great plant, with its many buildings, yards, and smoking stacks, lies just below the bluff on which stands the mansion.

During the middle 1850's Hegeler and a companion, Frederick W. Matthiessen, had come west from Pennsylvania in search of a suitable zinc-works site. Both were young mining engineers. They found what they wanted at La Salle, then experiencing a boom as a shipping point on the Illinois and Michigan Canal, which connected Chicago with the Illinois River at Peru. This factor, as well as the nearness of coal mines and the presence of zinc ore at Galena, caused them, in 1858, to establish their works at La Salle.

The firm grew rapidly. We are told that Hegeler and Matthiessen "carried on investigations and experiments leading to important discoveries which were embodied in patents on inventions, taken out jointly by both." The partners acquired coal mines, became financially interested in railroads, and began the manufacture of sulphuric acid.

Edward C. Hegeler House, La Salle, Built 1874.

Having become one of the wealthiest men in northern Illinois, Hegeler decided to erect a mansion suitable to his station. The same decision was reached by Frederick Matthiessen, and when the two houses were completed they won widespread admiration for their size and magnificence. About this time Matthiessen established the Western Clock Manufacturing Company and the La Salle Tool Company. Among his best-known philanthropies was his development of Deer Park, near La Salle. This property of 174.6 acres was given to the state of Illinois by the Matthiessen family in 1944. It is known as the Matthiessen State Park Nature Area.

Established in their spacious residence on the bluff above La Salle, Mr. and Mrs. Hegeler reared their children, entertained some of the leading men and women of the state, and reigned as one of the first families of La Salle. Two sons—Julius and Herman—established a second zinc smelter at Danville. This and the one at La Salle were the outstanding plants of their kind in America. Julius Hegeler also became a well-known Danville civic leader.

In its heyday the Hegeler abode was one of the show places of the Illinois River Valley. The house stood in the center of an estate occupying an entire city block. Fine shade trees spread their branches over well-kept lawns. Bubbling fountains, flower gardens, paths, and driveways added to the attractiveness of the place. From their small balcony porches or bay windows the Hegelers could see the broad, rolling surface of the Illinois River.

As he advanced in years Hegeler became more and more interested in religious and scientific problems. He was naturally of a scholarly disposition, and the mansion library was his favorite haunt. He met Dr. Paul Carus, a scholar and writer with similar views. The Open Court Publishing Company was established, with Dr. Carus, who had become Hegeler's son-in-law, as its head. Through this company the two men propounded their religious views.

From a biographical sketch of Hegeler in the *Official Reference Book of the Press Club of Chicago* (the zinc magnate having been a member of this club) we learn that the Open Court Publishing Company was founded for the purpose of bringing about "the free and full discussion of religious and psychological questions on the principle that the scientific world conception should be applied to religion. Mr. Hegeler believed in science, but he wished to preserve the religious spirit with all its serious endeavor, and in this sense he pleaded for the establishment of a religion of science and a science of religion."

From the La Salle mansion, with the assistance of a corps of editorial workers, translators, and printers, Hegeler sent out tracts, booklets, and magazines advancing his philosophical and religious beliefs. It is said that one of the reasons for this activity was to counteract the agnostic utterances of Colonel Robert Ingersoll, who lived in near-by Peoria.

Edward Hegeler died in 1910 at the age of seventy-five.

Historical Museum

AN INTERESTING example of the old mansions in Illinois which have been converted into historical museums is the venerable Tanner residence in Aurora, thriving century-old city on the Fox River. Located on the west side of the city, at Oak Avenue and Cedar Street, this old-fashioned mansion now houses the Aurora Historical Society and, as such, is replete with relics, souvenirs, and mementos of Aurora's early days; of the days when the city was a tiny sawmill settlement on the river known as McCarty's Mills.

The choice of this spacious, sturdy pre-Civil War mansion for a historical museum was fortunate, for the man who built it was not only one of the earliest pioneers of Aurora but one of the first settlers of Chicago. As a result, the house contains many articles of furniture from the Tanner household, thus adding to its appeal as a museum.

F. B. Marchialette

William A. Tanner House, Aurora, Built 1857.

171

Some of this furniture was brought to Aurora by the Tanners in sailing vessels on the Great Lakes.

From data compiled by Charles P. Burton, local historian and columnist of the *Aurora Beacon-News*, we learn that this residence was built in 1857 by William Augustus Tanner, one of the first hardware dealers of Aurora. The firm he founded more than a century ago, the Tanner Hardware Co., is still in existence. As a pioneer hardware dealer of Aurora, Tanner supplied tools to the settlers who built up civilization in the Fox River Valley.

But William Tanner was not new at the hardware business when he set up shop in Aurora. He acquired his first knowledge of it in Chicago, where he originally settled in the early 1830's after coming west from New York State. There he obtained employment in the hardware shop of King, Jones & Co.

However, Tanner did not stay in Chicago very long. In 1835 he struck out across the prairies and settled at McCarty's Mills. Here he remained for the rest of his life and here he played his role in the building of Aurora. His hardware business prospered and then, in 1841, he went back to New York State and married Anna Plum Makepeace. The couple returned to Aurora. By the middle 1850's Tanner was sufficiently well-to-do to build a mansion comparable to the best in Aurora.

Here the Tanners reared their children and entertained many important people of their day. The mansion is typical of the pre-Civil War period. It is of brick construction, two-and-a-half stories high, and has an octagonal cupola. There are seventeen rooms in the house and all are spacious and comfortable. This residence remained in the Tanner family until a few years ago when it was given to the Aurora Historical Society. The donors were Mrs. Martha T. Thornton, of Naperville, and Mrs. Mary T. Hopkins, of Kansas City, twin daughters of the Tanners.

As a museum the Tanner mansion, according to *Illinois: A Descriptive and Historical Guide*, contains a "grandfather's clock, Aurora's first piano and other pieces of early furniture brought by boat from Buffalo to Chicago and then hauled overland to Aurora. Home utensils, ornaments, intimate letters and other exhibits are arranged throughout the rooms to portray, in warmly personal terms, living conditions of early days. There is an excellent collection of pioneer portraits, an original Lincoln letter and a group of legal documents and memoirs of local historical significance."

In the Victorian atmosphere of this house the old-time residents of Aurora and the Fox River Valley hold a reunion once a year and recall the early days of their town and valley.

In the Lakes Country

A MAN who did much to further the cause of scientific agriculture in this country during pioneer days, and who even introduced progressive farming methods into Japan, was General Horace Capron, who established a home in Illinois. The old Capron house on a hill near Hebron, in the vicinity of the much-visited lakes region northwest of Chicago, has become a well-known residential landmark.

Horace Capron, whom one biographical reference work designates as "a public-spirited man of outstanding character, high ideals, great personal courage, and of courtly, distinguished bearing," built his house in 1850. But it was not until 1854 that he occupied the mansion, bringing to it a second wife, who was Margaret Baker of New York. Here the Caprons lived during the 1850's and supervised their large farm, which was almost a thousand acres in extent.

"During 1850 and early 1851 the 'Mansion' was built, the bricks and building materials being hauled from Milwaukee by slow ox teams," writes Kenneth K. Schaefer in a centennial history of Hebron, published in 1936. "The Capron house was a marvelous building for its day, and present-day visitors to the 'Mansion' cannot help being impressed with its spacious and multitudinous rooms, high ceilings, large fireplaces, solid mahogany spiral stairway and priceless glass chandeliers."

Horace Capron was born in Attleboro, Massachusetts, on August 31, 1804, the son of a physician who had served with distinction in the Revolutionary War. Another son, Seth Capron, was graduated from West Point in 1821 and for a time was stationed at Fort Dearborn, on the site of Chicago. Upon reaching maturity, Horace entered the cotton manufacturing business in Maryland and, following his first marriage, acquired a large farm. At this time he wrote a series of articles for the *American Farmer* magazine entitled "On the Renovation of Worn-Out Soils." He later became a leader in agricultural societies in Maryland.

During the years he lived in his northern Illinois mansion, Capron enlarged his experiments in progressive farming and helped to educate other farmers to improve their cultivation methods. This work was interrupted, however, by the outbreak of the Civil War in 1861. He was commissioned a lieutenant colonel of the 14th Illinois Cavalry, served in many campaigns, and later became a brigadier general. For a time he was adjutant to General Grant.

After the war, General Capron returned to his northern Illinois farm and later went to Washington, having been appointed United States

Horace Capron House, Hebron, Built 1850.

Commissioner of Agriculture. Then, in 1871, he resigned this post to accept an appointment from the Japanese government to introduce American farming methods into that country. After several years he returned to America and lived in Washington until his death in 1885.

When General Capron was living in his Hebron house after the Civil War, he entertained numerous distinguished persons, including General Grant. For his war services, Capron was awarded land by the government. On this tract the town of Capron grew up.

After General Capron left Hebron for Washington his mansion was occupied by his brothers, Newton and John. When they died, the Hebron house came into the possession of a number of successive owners, including George F. Harding, Sr., Halsey Fink, the Bates family, and George McClure. Here was born Granville Bates, well-known star of the "silent" movie days.

More recently the old Capron abode became the country home of Ross D. Siragusa, president of the Admiral Corporation of Chicago. And, in 1945, Mr. Siragusa sold the property to Royce A. Kelley, of Alden, Illinois.

Workman's Cottage

DURING the 1937 centennial of Knox College there was placed on a plain little workman's cottage near the smoky railroad shops in Galesburg a wooden marker containing the inscription: "Birthplace of Carl Sandburg. One of America's immortals. Placed by A. G." Although it is debatable whether a writer who is still alive can be designated an "immortal," most literary critics agree that if any living American writer has a chance to become immortal he is Carl Sandburg.

One noted literary critic, Harry Hansen, in his book, *Midwest Portraits*, touched on this point more than two decades ago (1923) or before Sandburg published his great master work on Abraham Lincoln. "In less than ten years," wrote Hansen, "Carl Sandburg has become a figure of national significance. Today he is invariably named as one of the four or five outstanding poets of America, and his influence toward a liberation from classical bondage and the development of wholesome American themes is felt among a host of followers. He has helped direct our thinking back to the primitive forces of our land; to the soil, human labor, the great industries, the masses of men. No matter what he writes in the future, the cumulative effect of his poems will survive and be of great influence in our land."

If Sandburg had written nothing at all after the publication of his numerous books of poetry, volumes which brought him national fame as the "Chicago Poet" or "the bard of the prairies," the house in which he was born would still be of widespread interest. But following the completion of his six-volume life of Lincoln, a work which made his name familiar throughout the Anglo-American world, the little workman's cottage in Galesburg has become one of America's literary landmarks. More and more visitors are coming to Galesburg each year to view the birthplace of the man who made Lincoln live again.

Although not of log construction, the house in which this man was born is as plain and humble as is the birthplace of his truly immortal hero. There is nothing to distinguish it from millions of other workmen's cottages that cluster near grim industrial works in cities throughout the country. It is a one-story frame dwelling with a gable roof, clapboard siding, front and rear door and a few windows. Nothing more. There is not even a small porch at the front entrance.

Here, then, in this small workman's cottage, was born Carl Sandburg, poet, ballad singer, columnist, lecturer, and Lincoln biographer. His birth occurred on January 6, 1878. He was one of the sons of August

Johnson, a Swedish immigrant who, upon arriving in Galesburg, discovered there were too many "Johnsons" among the Swedes there and changed his name to "Sandburg." It is said that a mixup in pay checks at the railroad shops caused Sandburg's father to make the change.

When Sandburg was a baby his father worked as a blacksmith for the Burlington railroad. He was a husky Swede who, it is said, could

C. C. Burford

Carl Sandburg House, Galesburg, Built 1870's.

not write English. In the little house he reared his family and took his place as one of the hundreds of honest, thrifty laborers who worked ten-hour shifts, six days a week, in the near-by railroad shops.

It was in the Galesburg cottage, at 311 East Third Street, that Carl Sandburg spent the first five or six years of his life. Each month, the elder Sandburg, out of his meager wages, had to pay rent for the use of the cottage. Later, however, August Sandburg bought a house of his own, and thereafter the family had little thought of the Third Street cottage. When Carl Sandburg was thirteen years old it was necessary for him to leave school and go to work, but he managed later to earn his way through Lombard and Knox colleges.

The poet's subsequent career, his work as a newspaperman on *The Chicago Daily News*, his first fame as the "Chicago Poet," his ballad singing, and finally the writing of his great, six-volume life of Lincoln—all these achievements are vividly told in *Carl Sandburg: A Study in Personality and Background* by Karl Detzer, published in 1941. Incidentally, it was recently recalled that Sandburg's first book of poetry, *In Reckless Ecstasy*, was issued by a Lombard, Illinois, printer in 1904, the author signing himself "Charles A. Sandburg." That Lombard printer was Philip G. Wright, father of Professor Quincy Wright, University of Chicago authority on international affairs and author of *A Study of War* and other books.

As might have been indicated by the closing phrase "Placed by A. G.," the wooden marker attached to the Sandburg cottage in 1937 was placed there by Mrs. Adda George of Galesburg. Since that time, she has organized the Carl Sandburg Association, which now numbers many prominent persons among its members. It was this association that purchased the Sandburg cottage and, after restoring it, opened it to the public as a museum of Sandburg and Lincoln relics and mementos.

Eccentric Inventor's Home

ONE of Illinois' most unusual houses, designed, built, and occupied by one of the most unusual characters in the recent history of the state, stands on the outskirts of Kewanee. Now owned by the city and maintained as a museum, this curious dwelling annually attracts hundreds of visitors who come to view the eccentric home of an eccentric man—a man who was an inventor, mathematician, artist, scholar, horticulturist, and recluse.

In this house lived Fred Francis, who died in 1926 at the age of seventy. As a dramatic climax to his strange career, he left an unusual will, which provided that his house and forty-acre estate, valued at $50,000, be given to Kewanee for a museum and public park—that is, under certain stipulations. The main one was that his body be cremated on a pyre of cordwood in his back yard and the ashes buried, coverless, in the earth.

If possessed of a romantic imagination, Francis was a realist, too. In his will he added that if the health authorities objected to the public cremation in his yard, his body was to be disposed of in a crematory. He summed up by saying if the city officials failed to carry out this provision of his will, his forty-acre estate and house were to be given to his alma mater, the University of Illinois. A graduate of this institution in 1878, he had displayed exceptional mathematical talents while there.

Shortly after the death of Francis, the Kewanee City Council, at a special meeting, provided for the carrying out of the terms of his will. One of these was that the house was to be opened only "when it is safe to do so without admitting flies or mice." It has been said that provisions of the will are being adhered to, but the "flies-and-mice" clause gives the caretakers many a bad time.

One of Francis' phobias was a particular horror of flies. To deal with this aversion, and also to indulge his tastes and hobbies, Francis designed an abode which is a unique example of the truism that the house reflects the man. Outstanding as an inventor, he conceived automatic-action doors and windows. When a window is opened, a screen automatically drops to keep out the flies. He obtained water from a huge cistern, "so designed that it was filtered, heated and syphoned into a marble bathroom."

Many household conveniences now in general use were enjoyed by Fred Francis in his dwelling years ago. He is said to have been one of the first to use air conditioning in a home. He accomplished this by

Fred Francis House, Kewanee, Built 1880's.

building a tunnel from his orchard to the house—which brought in fresh air, cooled by passage through the tunnel. A favorite haunt was his basement workshop, and here he operated his various machines with power obtained from a shaft and windmill arrangement.

At one corner of his abode stands a conservatory which he designed. It is heated in winter by a skillful arrangement of steam pipes. Here he nurtured his favorite plants and engaged in horticultural experiments.

In the various rooms of the house, rooms arranged at different levels, are displayed many paintings from the brush of the recluse. He had unusual gifts as an artist and showed discrimination as a collector of art objects. His ability as a mathematician is demonstrated in the dining room. Here, on one wall, are geometric symbols which Francis claimed were proof of the solution of various difficult mathematical problems. He is said to have been one of the outstanding mathematicians of the Midwest.

Obviously, Francis could not have built his house, with its many innovations, unless he had had the means to do so. His income was derived from royalties on patents, mostly in connection with watches—he had been employed for eleven years by the Elgin Watch Company.

The Octagon Mode

IN THE BURNHAM Library of Architecture at the Art Institute of Chicago may be found a small, rare, time-stained volume that was responsible for an exotic, but short-lived, architectural style throughout northeastern America in the years just before the Civil War. This book is *A Home for All; or, the Gravel Wall, and Octagon Mode of Building*, by O. S. Fowler of New York, who is identified on the title page as an "author of various works on phrenology." First published in 1849, this book was widely read in successive editions and resulted in the construction of octagon-shaped houses in many villages, towns, and cities from the Atlantic to the Mississippi.

Some of these eight-sided houses, with their curious V-shaped rooms, are still in existence. A number of them survive in Illinois, and one of the best of these, although not one of the most impressive, is the old Warren Clark house at Mendota. It is located on U. S. 34, at the west end of town, and is a unique residential landmark in that part of the state. Several generations of farmers, bringing their corn to Mendota, have wondered about the odd style of construction of this house.

Whether the builder of this dwelling, Warren Clark, was a follower of the phrenological writings of Professor O. S. Fowler has not been determined, but he must have known of Fowler when he built his abode in 1853. For at that time Professor Fowler was one of the most popular phrenologists in the United States, and his *Phrenological Almanac* was read by thousands. "Fowler's interests," says the *Dictionary of American Biography*, "were universal and he supposed himself able to solve the problems of every department of knowledge by means of 'phrenology and physiology' alone."

Discussing octagon houses in *Country Life in America* magazine (March, 1913), Fanny Hale Gardiner wrote: "Whether those who followed Fowler's teachings had the idea that there was any metaphysical connection between his diagram of our 'dome of thought' and his plan for a dwelling for our mortal body is not certain. There is no evidence that he intended a symbolical purpose in selecting a figure of eight sides rather than one of any other number."

Some clue as to what Professor Fowler had in mind when he designed the octagon-style house might be found in the introduction to his book where he wrote: "I kept asking myself, Why so little progress in architecture when there is so much in other matters? We continue to build in the same square form adopted by all past ages. Cannot some

180

radical change for the better be adopted, both as to the external form of houses and their interior arrangements? Why not take our pattern from Nature? Her forms are mostly spherical."

A comparison of the Warren Clark house with an etching of the residence built by Professor Fowler himself at Fishkill, New York, (which no longer exists) shows the similarity of the two dwellings. The professor's eight-sided house is, of course, more pretentious than the Mendota abode. When Warren Clark built his house he was a man of some means in the community. An early settler of La Salle County, he acquired land and helped to develop the region.

Set back on a landscaped lawn at the intersection of Washington Street and Iowa Avenue, the Warren Clark house is a two-story frame dwelling with a bay window on the south side and a small porch on the southeast wall. It has an almost flat roof of tin, with a chimney protruding from the center. The rooms of the house, some of them V-shaped, are plain, with pine trim. A walnut stairway leads to second-floor bedrooms.

Historic American Buildings Survey

Warren Clark House, Mendota, Built 1850's.

In a Picturesque Community

ON A HORSESHOE bend of the Rock River, some six miles northeast of Dixon, is one of the oldest, best preserved, and most attractive villages in Illinois. It is called Grand Detour, so-named by early French traders because of the "Great Bend" on which it stands. Having a population of no more than two hundred and being located away from main-traveled roads, Grand Detour is something of a "deserted village"; a white, elm-shaded, picket-fenced community of the type found in older New England regions.

Because of its picturesqueness, this little, century-old community has in recent years attracted a number of artists who have taken over some of the ancient red brick and white clapboard dwellings and converted them into studio homes. But Grand Detour is of interest to historical students, too, for the founders of the village, John Deere and Major Leonard Andrus, manufactured the first steel plows in the United States and thus played important roles in the development of American civilization.

In consequence, the two outstanding sights of Grand Detour are associated with these two men. One is the Major Leonard Andrus' Memorial, marking the site of the original Deere & Andrus plow factory, and the other is the home of John Deere. Situated in the center of the village under a huge, ancient elm and surrounded by a white picket fence, the Deere house, although built more than a hundred years ago, is remarkably well preserved and noteworthy for its interior furnishings, all of which are authentic and of the John Deere period.

A native of Rutland, Vermont, where he was born on February 7, 1804, John Deere came west in 1837 and settled at Grand Detour. He set up a blacksmith shop and the following year he built his house and brought his family to Grand Detour. Both he and Major Andrus, who also was from Vermont, succeeded in bringing other settlers from the Green Mountain State to Grand Detour and soon the village was a thriving community.

Since its two best-known citizens were Vermonters, as were many of its first settlers, it was inevitable that Grand Detour should grow and develop in the manner of a New England village. Like innumerable old Vermont communities, Grand Detour has wide, unpaved streets, footpaths instead of sidewalks, houses set far back on spacious lawns, windlass wells, picket fences, and massive old trees that arch over the streets and in summer clothe the white village in a mantle of green.

182

When Grand Detour was at the height of its boom in the middle 1840's, due mainly to the presence of the Deere & Andrus plow factory, the village contained an estimated population of a thousand. The number declined, however, when railroads appeared in the late 1840's and by-passed Grand Detour. It was in 1847 that John Deere sold his interest to Major Andrus and moved to Moline, where he established a larger plow works than the original factory.

With the departure of John Deere, his house acquired a new owner. It continued to be occupied as a dwelling through the Civil War period.

John Deere House, Grand Detour, Built 1838.

In later years, an unsuccessful attempt was made to purchase it by Deere's son, Charles, who had become president of the Deere company. The house did come back into the Deere family, however, some years after the death of Charles Deere when it was acquired by his daughter, Mrs. William Butterworth, of Moline.

Appreciating the historic value of this house, which is a simple, dignified, two-story frame dwelling with a classic portico, Mrs. Butterworth carefully furnished its rooms with maple and walnut furniture, fine china and pottery, pictorial wallpaper, hooked rugs, old lithographs, mid-Victorian bric-a-brac, and other household articles of the 1840's.

Amid Unusual Rural Beauty

RECALLING her girlhood days in northern Illinois, the late Jane Addams, founder of Hull House in Chicago and world-famous humanitarian, once wrote: "These early recollections are set in a scene of rural beauty, unusual, at least, for Illinois. The prairie around the village was broken into hills, one of them crowned by pine woods, grown up from a bag full of Norway pine seeds sown by my father in 1844, the very year he came to Illinois, a testimony perhaps that the most vigorous pioneers gave at least an occasional thought to beauty."

Continuing, she said: "The banks of the mill stream rose into high bluffs too perpendicular to be climbed without skill, and containing caves of which one at least was so black that it could not be explored without the aid of a candle. . . . My stepbrother and I carried on games and crusades which lasted week after week, and even summer after summer, as only free-ranging country children can do."

It was in this idyllic setting that Jane Addams spent her childhood and young womanhood. The house in which she was born, one of the oldest in the little village of Cedarville, some six miles north of Freeport, still stands in its grove of elms and has become a revered historic shrine, much visited by admirers of the great humanitarian.

When she grew to maturity Jane Addams remembered her happy, "free-ranging" childhood days at Cedarville, and it was in part this memory that caused her to become interested in underprivileged children of the foreign districts of Chicago. Deciding to help these children, to give them a place to play and an opportunity to develop into good Americans, Miss Addams founded Hull House in 1889.

Miss Addams was but two years old when her mother died and after this her father became the guiding star of her young girlhood. Eight years after the death of his wife John H. Addams married again, this time to the widow of William Haldeman, a Freeport businessman. The second Mrs. Addams was an educated, accomplished woman and her little stepdaughter, Jane, became attached to her. When she became mistress of the Cedarville house the new wife brought along her two sons, Harry and George Haldeman.

In these early years John H. Addams was an outstanding personage of northern Illinois. Honest, self-educated, idealistic, and a hard worker, John Addams had prospered as the owner of a gristmill adjoining his home at Cedarville. He was elected to the state legislature, helped to establish the Republican Party, was a close friend of Abraham Lin-

Raymond Folgate

Jane Addams House, Cedarville, Built 1854.

coln's, organized the "Addams Guards" during the Civil War and helped to found the Galena and Chicago Union Railroad which was later consolidated with the Chicago & North Western Railway.

"By that time [in 1849, when Cedarville was platted] John Addams was on the highroad to prosperity," wrote the late Professor James Weber Linn in his *Jane Addams: A Biography*. Linn, who was a nephew of Jane Addams', tells us that "in 1854 he built for his increasing family a wide, two-story-and-attic, gray-brick house, in the simple, oblong architecture of the day." Here Jane Addams was born on September 6, 1860. And here she was living when her father died in 1881 at the age of fifty-nine.

Subsequently the old Addams homestead, in its grove of pines and elms at the base of the steep cliff on Cedar Creek, became the property of Marcet Haldeman, daughter of Miss Addams' stepbrother, Harry Haldeman, who had become a physician and banker of Girard, Kansas. It was in the Addams home that Marcet Haldeman was married to Emanuel Julius, a writer. Under the firm name of E. Haldeman-Julius, the two publish the five-cent "blue books" at Girard, Kansas.

Still in sound condition after almost a century, the old Addams homestead, now privately owned, retains much of the atmosphere of pioneer times. It has been furnished with many fine period pieces—articles of furniture and other household belongings contemporaneous with the girlhood days of Jane Addams.

Abode of a Statesman

DURING the early part of the nineteenth century there lived in Maine a large family whose sons, upon reaching maturity, played important roles in the history of various states and the nation at large. This was the Washburn family, established at Livermore, Maine, by Israel and Martha Washburn. One of the best known of the sons was Elihu Benjamin Washburne, who, early in life, attached an "e" to his name after his English forebears. As a congressman from Illinois, as Secretary of State during President Grant's administration, and as United States minister to France, Elihu B. Washburne was one of the outstanding men of the 1870's and 1880's.

In view of such a career, his home at Galena, Illinois, which he built about a century ago, is one of the principal sights in a city rich in historical sights. It was in the library of the Washburne house that General Grant received news of his election as President of the United States in 1868. This news was conveyed over telegraph wires into the Washburne abode and marked the first time in American history that a presidential candidate himself received such welcome news by telegraph. It was welcome news, too, to Congressman Washburne, for he had long been a close friend and champion of Ulysses S. Grant.

When Grant arrived in Galena in 1860 to work in his brother's eather store, Washburne was representing that community and that region in Congress. The two were introduced and became friends. Upon the outbreak of the Civil War, many Galena men volunteered for service and a company of these volunteers was drilled by Grant on the lawn adjacent to Congressman Washburne's house. Subsequently, Washburne sponsored the bills in Congress that brought promotions to his friend Grant—lieutenant general and, later, general. And after the war, Washburne was a leader in the campaign to elect Grant President.

The Congressman was equally devoted to Abraham Lincoln. It is said that he used "his talents in Congress to aid his personal and political friend Lincoln." He is on record as having been the only person to welcome President-elect Lincoln at the train upon the latter's secret arrival in Washington for the inauguration of 1861. This secrecy was put into effect following rumors of a plot to assassinate the President-elect.

After General Grant became President in 1868, Elihu Washburne left his home in Galena and went to live in Washington. He was appointed Secretary of State in Grant's cabinet and, later, was named United States minister to France. In that capacity he saw the downfall of Napoleon III's empire and the establishment of the Paris Commune. His two volumes of memoirs, *Recollections of a Minister to France, 1869-1877*, are regarded as valuable historical records of France in the days of the Commune. On his retirement from public life, Elihu Washburne took up residence in Chicago and devoted the remainder of his days to literary and historical pursuits.

The residence in Galena which remains today as a memorial to Elihu Washburne is believed to have been built between 1845 and 1850,

Historic American Buildings Survey

Elihu B. Washburne House, Galena, Built 1840's.

according to the Historic American Buildings Survey. It is known that Washburne was married in 1845 to Adèle Gratiot, descendant of French settlers from St. Louis, and the presumption is that he built his house in the years immediately afterward. It is a two-story brick abode and resembles Greek Revival residences of Southern plantations—that is with a two-story "temple" portico.

The records show that in 1882 the Washburne house was sold to Thomas Sheean and that a porch was added to the north side of the house that same year. In 1931 title to the property was conveyed to Frank T. Sheean, member of the same Sheean family and judge of the Circuit Court. Although a century old, this historic house is well preserved and is often visited by sight-seers and students of history.

A Gift from the People

AS ALMOST everyone in the state knows, two of the most famous old houses in Illinois are the Abraham Lincoln home in Springfield and the Ulysses S. Grant home in Galena. Each is associated with one of the nation's greatest men and both are now owned and maintained by the state of Illinois as historic shrines. Thousands of tourists from all parts of the country visit these dwellings each year, obtaining a glimpse in them of the home life of two men who played vitally important parts in the history of the United States.

The Grant home is the principal sight of Galena, picturesque old-time city in a hollow of the hills at the extreme northwest corner of the state, not far from the Mississippi River. This city was once a booming river town, located on the Galena River, and had its rise with the discovery of lead in the vicinity. But with the coming of the railroads in the 1850's, Galena declined and soon lost its position as a lead-producing center. Still standing, however, are the fine old mansions and houses of the men who made fortunes in the lead mines. These, as well as the Grant home, attract sight-seers to the city from near and far.

It was just after the close of the Civil War that General Grant, who had helped win the war for the Union cause and who was therefore the hero of the day in the North, was presented with the spacious, two-story brick residence in Galena that was in after-years to become a memorial to him. Here the Grants lived until 1868 when the General was elected President of the United States.

Just why a house in Galena should be chosen and presented to General Grant is easily explained. It was simply that Galena was Grant's city of adoption. He had gone there before the outbreak of the Civil War and at a time when he was low in funds and needed a job. For some years before this, he had served in the Army. Upon leaving the Army, he secured a $600-a-year job as clerk in a leather goods store operated by two of his younger brothers in Galena.

Still standing, this store, at 120 Main Street, is now one of the sights of Galena. Another is the modest home which Grant and his family occupied when they first came to Galena; when Grant was an obscure retired Army lieutenant. This dwelling is at 121 High Street, located on a hill slope above downtown Galena. Here Grant and his wife and four children were living when Lincoln was elected President and Fort Sumter was bombarded.

As a former professional soldier, one who had been graduated from

West Point and who had fought in the Mexican War, the Galena store clerk offered his services to the War Department. Response to his offer was slow in coming. In the meantime, Grant trained volunteers for the Army and his drill ground was the lawn of the Elihu B. Washburne house in Galena. Subsequently, Grant was commissioned a colonel of the 21st Regiment of Illinois Infantry by Governor Yates. Thus began his Civil War career, a career that brought him international renown.

At the close of the war, when General Grant had accepted the gift mansion from the people of his adopted city, he found himself in possession of one of the show places of Galena. It had been built in 1857 by Alexander Jackson, an influential and successful citizen of the boom town. In obtaining it as a gift for General Grant, the citizens are said to have paid $15,000. This sum included the furnishings of the house.

"The new home was on a high hill across the river on the East side, almost opposite the first home," writes Florence Gratiot Bale in her *Galena's Yesterdays*. She continues: "The Grants established themselves

Herbert Georg Studio

Ulysses S. Grant House, Galena, Built 1857.

in this sightly and comfortable house, and renewed the friendships of early days, and General Grant showed his intention of making it his permanent home by bringing his war trophies with him."

Mrs. Bale tells us that "people in the town entertained the Grants at dinners and other social affairs; all the ladies made formal calls on Mrs. Grant and once more the old town felt Grant was a citizen of Galena. His official duties took him to Washington and he was away a great deal of the time, but his legal home was always considered Galena. In 1868, his country gave him the greatest honor it can confer; he was elected President of the United States, and the family left their home and removed to the White House in Washington."

After the Grants left, the residence in Galena was occupied by H. H. Houghton and his wife. Mr. Houghton was editor of the *Galena Gazette* and at one time had been postmaster of the town. When Grant completed his second term as President, he and his family came back to the Galena mansion. Here he was living when, in 1880, he was prevailed upon to become a candidate for President once more. Upon losing the campaign to Garfield, ex-President Grant moved to New York. His last days were spent writing his *Personal Memoirs*, which became a best seller. He died July 23, 1885.

Following the departure of the Grants, their brick residence was rented to the Rev. Ambrose Smith, who was pastor of the South Presbyterian Church of Galena. Subsequently, the house was occupied by David Nash Corwith and his family and, later, by the C. C. Matheys. It was then given to the city in 1904.

The house today, open free to the public, is filled with furniture and other household belongings of the Grants. On the plate rail in the dining room are dishes which were used in the White House during Grant's administration. This room also contains the silver used in the White House. The dining-table centerpiece was made by Mrs. Grant herself. It is an arrangement of bananas, oranges, pears, and grapes, carefully preserved in wax and still bright in their glass bell jar after more than three-quarters of a century.

"The Larches"

DURING the seventy-five years it has been standing in its grove of larch trees a mile outside of Onarga, small city in the eastern part of Illinois, the Allan Pinkerton house has given rise to more conjectures and legends than perhaps any other dwelling in the state. This was undoubtedly caused by the career of the man who built the house, for Allan Pinkerton, as this country's earliest and best-known private detective, had worked on many sensational crimes and plots during the Civil War period and later and, besides, had written eighteen widely read books telling of his experiences.

In a paper read several years ago before the Lincoln Group of Chicago, Clint Clay Tilton, a Danville historian, said of Pinkerton and his house: "Here [near Onarga] he caused to be built the square house which he termed his 'villa,' but which is known locally in this day as the Pinkerton 'Whoopee house.' . . . The villa never was used as a family home but was the scene of many a high carnival when he went there with his cronies for days of relaxation. Within the walls of the historic house leaders in sports, the stage, writers of note and painters of national reputation would gather as his guests, during which time the Stars and Stripes would flutter from the flagpole atop the lookout tower in the center of the building."

Others of less repute came to this house, too, Tilton declared. Referring to the various rooms of the dwelling, he says: "One . . . was made soundproof, where he held interviews with mysterious individuals from time to time, giving rise to the tradition that ex-convicts frequently found a haven there until they could accustom themselves to their new freedom."

When this country dwelling was built in 1873, Pinkerton—or "The Eye," as he was widely called—was already at the height of his career and had amassed a considerable fortune as head of a private detective agency of national scope. Twelve years earlier he first attracted widespread attention as the personal bodyguard of President-elect Abraham Lincoln during the sensational "Baltimore Scare." It was Pinkerton's belief, based on the evidence of one of his operatives, Timothy Webster, that Lincoln was to be assassinated in Baltimore. So "The Eye" arranged for Lincoln to change trains secretly. This was done and he arrived safely in Washington.

At the time he built the Onarga house, Pinkerton was a resident of Chicago. It was there, in fact, that he began his career as a professional detective. Born in Glasgow, Scotland, in 1819, Allan Pinkerton came to Chicago in 1842, and a year later moved to the Scotch settlement of Dundee on the Fox River, where he set up a cooper's shop. In 1846 he was made a deputy sheriff of Kane County after discovering and helping round up a gang of counterfeiters.

During this time, being an ardent abolitionist, he also served as a "foreman" of the Underground Railway, his cooper's shop being a "sta-

Chicago Daily News

Allan Pinkerton House, Near Onarga, Built 1873.

tion" of the railway. By 1850 he was living in Chicago and serving on the city's police force as its first detective. He later organized a private detective agency, said to be America's first such organization, and helped to solve several sensational express robberies.

After the "Baltimore Scare" and following service with General George B. McClellan during the Civil War, Allan Pinkerton, in 1864, acquired a 254-acre farm on the outskirts of Onarga. It was on this tract he built his villa nine years later. In landscaping the grounds around the house, "The Eye" planted many larch trees, as well as other types of evergreens, and in time his estate was called "The Larches."

It became a show place of Iroquois County in the 1870's and '80's. Writing of this estate for the Historic American Buildings Survey, Loren

Van Degraft said: "He created on the prairies of Illinois a replica of a gentleman's estate he had known when a boy in Scotland. The larch trees were imported from Scotland and were set in orderly rows along the drives of the estate. Along these drives were planted thousands of flowers in beds that were always neat and orderly. Guards were stationed at the gates, and visitors who drove their horses along the drive faster than a walk were fined five dollars for raising dust that would settle on the flowers."

Some idea of what "The Larches" was like in its prime was obtained from an old Onarga resident, John Nichols, who served as a kind of major-domo of the Pinkerton estate. He reports that the estate contained a fish pond and swimming pool, a race track and numerous outbuildings. These latter included a great barn called "Big Jumbo" where between forty and fifty Indian ponies were housed, a wine cellar called "The Snuggery," which was connected with the villa by an underground passage, a milk house, root cellar, several smaller barns, and a group of greenhouses. The sloping walls of "The Snuggery" were decorated with murals of heroic Scots attired in kilts.

The villa, now showing signs of decay, is a frame building, one-and-a-half stories high, with a windowed cupola on its roof. Originally, it contained verandas on all four sides. A wide hall runs through the center of the house and on each side are bedrooms and living rooms. Still to be seen on the walls of the central hall are the murals of Civil War scenes of which Major Pinkerton was so proud. Running water for the villa was furnished by a large wind engine.

"It was a lively place on week ends," recalled old John Nichols. "Major Pinkerton would come down from Chicago on Fridays with a group of friends and go back on Monday morning. They would arrive on an Illinois Central train, getting off at a special stop alongside the estate. There were always three cooks on duty and the pay roll, I distinctly remember, ran to $1,200 a month. Yes, sir, it was a great place while it lasted, but after Major Pinkerton died, in 1884, it gradually declined. And now it is but a mere shadow of what it once was."

Swiss Cottage

AN OUTSTANDING example of exotic architecture in Illinois is the Swiss Cottage at Rockford. Standing there for more than three-quarters of a century, this authentic reproduction of an Alpine chalet is one of the principal sights of the big city on the Rock River. During World War II many of the thousands of soldiers at near-by Camp Grant viewed it on their walks through the city—just as it was glimpsed by soldiers from the same camp during World War I. Recently, the Rockford Park District voted funds for the care and maintenance of this unusual landmark.

Not only is the Swiss Cottage, which stands at 411 Kent Street, on a bluff overlooking Kent Creek, of absorbing interest to architectural students, but it survives as a memorial to one of Rockford's noted personages of the 1870's and '80's. This man was Robert H. Tinker, who was elected mayor of Rockford in 1875. A cultured, widely traveled individual, Tinker was one of the "fathers" of the Rockford Grand Opera House, now gone, and also was instrumental in establishing the city's system of sixty-three attractive parks.

In the many world-wide travels he made with his wife, Robert Tinker is said to have become impressed with a chalet he saw in Switzerland and thereupon to have decided to build a home in this style when he returned to America. His determination was carried out and in the early 1870's the Swiss Cottage was built for him.

With its broad, low gables, overhanging eaves, and ornate galleries, it is an authentic reproduction of the type of dwelling so familiar in the Alps. At the time the cottage was built it stood on the attractive grounds of the Manny estate—one of the best-known estates in Rockford.

Into his comfortable frame house, with its twenty-six rooms, Tinker brought his large collection of books. This collection included hundreds of volumes which he acquired when Rockford's first community library was auctioned in 1865. All of the Tinker books are housed in the library, one of the most impressive rooms in the cottage. It is circular in shape and its ceiling reaches to the full height of the house. A circular staircase of intricately carved wood serves the second-floor balcony in the library.

In all the rooms of his house, Tinker installed the many antiques, art objects, curios, and souvenirs which he had collected in his travels. Here, too, are rare oil paintings, as well as fine examples of period furniture. Among the latter is a settee on which Abraham Lincoln is said

H. Bruckner

Robert H. Tinker House, Rockford, Built 1870's.

to have sat. Another interesting item here is an early oil portrait of Mark Twain.

The Lincoln settee originally came from the mansion of John H. Manny, who moved to Rockford in 1853 with a reaper he had invented, began the wholesale manufacture of his invention, prospered, and built for himself a mansion which stood across Kent Creek from the Swiss Cottage. When Cyrus H. McCormick sued Manny, charging infringement of the McCormick patent, the Rockford inventor was defended in the federal court at Cincinnati by Abraham Lincoln. Manny was cleared of the accusation. It was at this time that Lincoln is alleged to have used the settee in the Manny residence.

When Robert Tinker died, the Swiss Cottage was occupied by his widow. Here she lived for many years, surrounded by treasures that had been collected over a period of half a century. With her death, the cottage and five acres of landscaped ground around it passed to the Rockford Park District.

"Indian Terrace"

WHEN, several decades ago, the century-old Sanford residence in Rockford was acquired by a prominent business and civic leader of that city, Mr. Ralph Hinchliff, a corps of workmen and skilled artisans immediately went to work on a restoration of the house and the wide lawns around it. Today, the quaint old Sanford home, with its board-and-batten siding, its windowed cupola, its fanciful eave brackets, and other details of nineteenth century architecture, is an outstanding historic show place, widely known as "Indian Terrace." Because of its authentic mid-Victorian atmosphere, both outside and inside, Indian Terrace is attracting the attention of an ever-growing number of historical and architectural students, as well as "period" decorators and antiquarians. Members of the Illinois State Historical Society, at their forty-eighth annual meeting in Rockford, foregathered at Indian Terrace and heard the story of this venerable landmark of northern Illinois.

As Indian Terrace, however, is the private home of Mr. and Mrs. Hinchliff, it has none of the discomforts, the stuffiness, and overcrowding usually associated with mid-Victorian interiors. Here, Mr. and Mrs. Hinchliff, both of whom are historically minded, with a fine perception of artistic requirements, have created an atmosphere of the past without losing any of the comforts of the present. As those who know agree, this is the secret of successful old-house restoration. In this picturesque mansion, then, the Hinchliffs can, and do, continue the traditions of hospitality and gracious living introduced here a century ago by the builder of the house, Goodyear Asa Sanford.

It has been definitely ascertained that Goodyear Sanford built this home—now located at 505 North Main Street—in 1847. The site on which it was constructed was a sizable tract of land that Sanford and his cousin, Worcester A. Dickerman, had acquired and which included an ancient Indian mound. This latter gave rise to the present name of "Indian Terrace." When their home was completed, Mr. and Mrs. Sanford immediately gave it an atmosphere of generous hospitality by staging an elaborate house-warming party, climaxed by a magnificent dinner. Thus was begun a tradition of hospitality in the Sanford residence that continues to the present time. Here, too, the Sanfords early fostered cultural activities, the city's first literary circle, the Monday Group, having been formed in this house in 1877 by the second Mrs. Sanford. In addition, Goodyear Sanford devoted much time to his two hobbies— animal pets and flower gardens.

When Mr. and Mrs. Hinchliff obtained the old Sanford residence, they installed in its many rooms their collections of art objects, antiques, and mementos gathered over the years in all quarters of the globe. The result, however, is not a museum. Each room is comfortable and livable. A descendant of the Harlan family of colonial Virginia, and of the Cox family, members of which were prominent in the early history of Kentucky, Mrs. Hinchliff possesses many prized family heirlooms, as does Mr. Hinchliff of his ancestors who came over on the *Mayflower*.

But Indian Terrace is more than just a restored mid-Victorian mansion. It is situated in the midst of an attractively landscaped estate, shaded by numerous old maples, elms, and catalpas. Old brick walks, bordered by tulips and other flowers, connect the various outbuildings— the quaint guest house, the greenhouses, and the garage. On the basis of a century-old garden plan, drawn by Goodyear Sanford's old Scotch gardener, Mr. Hinchliff was able to restore the "congress boot" design of the Sanford garden and to rebuild the curious serpentine wall along one side of it.

Herzog

Goodyear Asa Sanford House, Rockford, Built 1847.

Fox River French Chateau

REMINISCENT of a chateau in La Perche, that district of France famous for its Percheron horses, is the gray stone mansion in the little village of Wayne in northern Illinois, a mansion widely known as Dunham Castle. Modeled after a French chateau, this residence has been a landmark of the Fox River Valley for more than half a century, being particularly associated with the introduction of Percheron horses into America. Although Percherons no longer roam the pastures around it, the castle continues to be an equestrian center, for on its grounds each year is held the Dunham Woods Horse Show, and here, too, are staged annual hunts and other equestrian events. It is also the nucleus of a colony of socially prominent Chicago gentleman farmers, and among guests here in the past have been numerous members of European royal houses.

In a setting not unlike that of provincial France, with great old elms bordering roadsides and stone gates marking the entrances to estates, Dunham Castle stands as a memorial to the man who built it—Mark Dunham. It stands, too, as a reminder of Mark Dunham's role in the history of American agriculture—the introduction and long-continued breeding of Percheron horses; sturdy draft horses which helped break the soil of the western prairies and aided the advancement of civilization in the Midwest. As a breeder of horses Mark Dunham in his time was visited by horse fanciers not only from all parts of America, but from many European countries as well.

He was America's leading importer and breeder of Percherons during the latter half of the nineteenth century. He brought them over by the shipload and transported them in special trains to Wayne. Old residents of Du Page County say that the whinnying of the Percherons could be heard for miles when they ate their first mouthful of green grass after weeks of travel by boat and train. According to one story Mark Dunham turned down an offer of $20,000 for a colt on the New York dock and this colt in a few years became the most famous Percheron in America. His name was Brilliant. He was the ancestor of a long line of blue-ribbon Percherons.

Once when Mark Dunham was on a business trip in Normandy he was asked about American western ponies by Rosa Bonheur, famous French painter of animals. She said she would like to paint some of them. On his next trip to France, Dunham brought along two ponies for the painter. She was so gratified over this generous gift that she

F. B. Marchialette

Mark Dunham House, Wayne, Built 1880.

made two paintings of Percherons which Dunham had purchased and presented them to him. These are still in the possession of the Dunham family. Additional prized possessions of the family are numerous bronze statues of horses made by famous French sculptors.

Having acquired a fortune as a breeder and importer of horses, Mark Dunham decided to build a large house suitable to his tastes. The castle was erected in 1880. It immediately won the admiration of residents of the Fox River Valley and visitors from Chicago and other points. Although modeled after a French chateau, the mansion has an interior more in keeping with the late Victorian era. Still in the house today are the furniture and other household articles used in Mark Dunham's time.

Much like that of any well-to-do horse breeder of France, Mark Dunham built his castle on an ancestral estate. For the land on which it stands was acquired by his father, Solomon Dunham, in 1842. A native of New York State, Solomon Dunham had come west with his family, traveling by way of a flatboat on the Ohio River and a covered wagon across Illinois. He acquired three hundred acres of land near the Fox River, paying $1.25 an acre, and built a log cabin. He was one of the founders of Wayne. In time he built himself a brick house, made from clay on the spot, and this house is today the Dunham Woods Riding Club.

In the years when Mr. and Mrs. Mark Dunham lived in the castle they entertained many notable personages. Among the earliest of these were the Infanta Eulalia of Spain and the Duke of Beragua. The castle was the scene of a brilliant wedding when Belle Dunham, daughter of Solomon, was married to Count Adimari-Morelli, of Italy. One of the latest royal visitors was Crown Princess Juliana of the Netherlands, who was a guest there on her visit to Chicago a decade ago.

Living in the shadow of the castle are a number of prominent Chicagoans, among them the novelist, Arthur Meeker, and Corwith Hamill. And, in the fields around the castle where blooded Percherons once pastured, tractors are used to cultivate the soil.

Birthplace of a Novelist

IN THE OPINION of many literary critics, Ernest Hemingway is among the foremost American writers of our time. They claim he will occupy a permanent place in American literature. If this is the case, it follows that the house in which Hemingway was born and where he spent his early childhood should be of interest to many people, and especially to devotees of his writings. That house still stands. It is one of the older dwellings of Oak Park, well-to-do village on the western border of Chicago.

The Hemingway home is located at 339 North Oak Park Avenue. Here Ernest Hemingway was born on July 21, 1898. And here he spent the first six years of his life. When he was six years old, his parents

Chicago Daily News

Ernest Hemingway House, Oak Park, Built 1890.

moved to another house near by, at 600 North Kenilworth Avenue, and it was in this dwelling that the future novelist grew to maturity. After graduating from Oak Park High School, young Hemingway left Oak Park and went out into the world to achieve fame as a writer.

The house in which he was born was built in 1890. It is a typical middle-class Queen Anne dwelling of the late Victorian era. Of frame construction and two stories high, it is marked by a corner tower with a conical roof. Originally, there was an open porch at the front, but this has been replaced by an inclosed porch. Several big trees planted by Ernest Hemingway's father shade the house in summer. On the inside, the rooms are large and comfortable and fireplaces warm some of them. The novelist was born in the south bedroom on the second floor.

His parents were both well-known Oak Parkers. His father was the late Dr. Clarence Edmonds Hemingway, who had practiced medicine in the Chicago suburb for almost half a century. Dr. Hemingway's father, Anson Tyler Hemingway, was a pioneer real-estate man of Chicago, having settled there after serving in the Civil War. The novelist's mother, Mrs. Grace Hall Hemingway, in her earlier years was a musician and vocal teacher and later became a painter. Many of her oils and water colors have been exhibited in Chicago.

The house in which the author of *For Whom the Bell Tolls* and other novels spent his earliest years was built by Mrs. Hemingway's father, Ernest Hall, who, with his brother-in-law, William L. Randall, conducted a wholesale cutlery house in Chicago—the second such firm to be established in the city. In the late 1880's Hall moved to Oak Park and, after living in a rented house, built the Oak Park Avenue abode.

Early in life Ernest Hemingway discovered the world of literature in the library of his grandfather's house. And not far from his house he discovered the delights of the outdoor life, of fishing and hiking and hunting. We are told that his father was fond of the outdoors and took Ernest on many hikes along the Des Plaines River and through Thatcher's Woods, pointing out birds, flowers, and trees to the youngster.

It was from the house on Oak Park Avenue that Ernest Hemingway first went to school. His mother took him to a private kindergarten conducted by Mrs. Helen Thane Raymond and here the future author learned to read and write. Much of his early education, of course, came from his parents, both of whom encouraged his interest in the world of books, art, and music.

"Ganymede"

IN EXISTENCE for almost half a century, the Eagle's Nest Art Colony on the attractive, wooded banks of the Rock River, in the Black Hawk country of northern Illinois, is one of the best-known art colonies of the Midwest. Here, during the heyday of the community, gathered writers, artists, and sculptors who were nationally known and who did much to develop a native American literature and art. One member of the group, Lorado Taft, executed the giant statue of Black Hawk that towers above the Rock River just north of Eagle's Nest.

In the center of this colony, which is located across the river from the town of Oregon, stands a comfortable old white stone residence that is regarded with reverence by artists and writers who visit it today.

For here lived the founder and benefactor of the community, Wallace Heckman, who was a distinguished Chicago lawyer, connoisseur of the arts, and business manager of the University of Chicago. In his later years he became vice-president of the Chicago Surface Lines. Although a man of business affairs, Wallace Heckman had an appreciation of the arts which few Chicago men of his time could equal.

That he should establish an art colony on the Rock River seems natural, since this region, with its riverside bluffs, woodlands, and rolling country, is one of the most scenic in the northern part of the state. But Heckman was not the first to discover its attractiveness. A famous American woman writer seems to have been the first to call attention to the charm of the Rock River country. She was Margaret Fuller, one of the Concord group of writers. She visited this region in 1843 and described it in one of her books, *At Home and Abroad*.

But she did more than this. She gave a name to this spot, calling it Eagle's Nest because of a tall, dead cedar tree upon which eagles nested. Here, too, on July 4, 1843, she composed one of her best-known poems, "Ganymede to His Eagle." And another thing she did was to name a spring near the riverside "Ganymede's Spring." What brought Margaret Fuller to this place originally was that here lived a cousin of hers, one of the early settlers of Ogle County.

As a consequence of this visit by Margaret Fuller in the early days, Wallace Heckman, when he set up the art colony here, formally called it Eagle's Nest. And upon completion of his residence in 1893, he named it "Ganymede." He had earlier visited the Rock River country, was impressed with its scenic beauties and had bought a thirteen-acre tract here for his country home.

Then, five years after being established in his spacious house on Rock River, Wallace Heckman invited a group of Chicago writers, artists, and sculptors to spend their summers on the grounds of his estate and provided cabins for them. They accepted the invitation, and from that year the popularity of the colony grew.

In the original group who came in 1898 were Lorado Taft, sculptor; Ralph Clarkson, Charles Francis Browne, and Oliver Dennett Grover, artists; Hamlin Garland, Henry B. Fuller, and Horace Spencer Fiske, writers; Irving K. and Allen B. Pond, architects; Clarence Dickinson, organist; and James Spencer Dickerson, secretary of the University of Chicago.

In his widely read book, *A Daughter of the Middle Border*—a book, by the way, which was written in the guest room of the Heckman residence—Hamlin Garland described at some length the early days of the colony. Here, in this idyllic setting, Garland began a romance with Lorado Taft's sister, Zulime, which led to their marriage. Having an attractive personality, Miss Taft was one of the most popular members of the original group.

"The camp," wrote Garland, "consisted of a small kitchen cabin, a dining tent, a group of cabins, and one or two rude studios to which the joyous offhand manners of the Fine Arts Building had been transferred. It was, in fact, a sylvan settlement of city dwellers—a colony of artists, writers, and teachers out for a summer vacation."

Describing the house, Garland wrote: "The Heckman home, which the campers called 'The Castle,' or 'The Manor House,' a long, two-story building of stone which stood on the southern end of the Bluff, overlooked what had once been Black Hawk's Happy Hunting Ground. It was not in any sense a chateau, but it pleased Wallace Heckman's artist-tenants to call it so and by contrast with their cookhouse it did, indeed, possess something like grandeur."

In later years many other famous writers and artists visited Eagle's Nest, among them William Vaughn Moody, Ralph Pierson, Bert Leston Taylor, Harriet Monroe, Lucy Fitch Perkins, George Barr McCutcheon, John T. McCutcheon, Dr. James H. Breasted, Mrs. Laura McAdoo Triggs, Edgar A. Bancroft, Charles R. Crane, and I. K. Friedman. Here, too, came Robert Burns Peattie and his novelist wife, Elia, who brought with them their two sons, Donald Culross and Roderick, both of whom were to become nationally-known writers.

Since the death, several years ago, of Ralph Clarkson, painter and one of the original members of the colony, there has been little activity at Eagle's Nest. Throughout the life of the colony, Mrs. Heckman as-

Wallace Heckman House, Near Oregon, Built 1893.

sisted her husband in providing hospitality for the guest writers and artists.

In the years since the Eagle's Nest colony was established, numerous prominent Chicagoans have acquired farms and estates in this vicinity. One of the largest of these tracts is the 4,600-acre Sinnissippi Farms, originally owned by the late Colonel Frank O. Lowden, former governor of Illinois. Just north of Eagle's Nest is the farm of Hal O'Flaherty, foreign editor of *The Chicago Daily News*. Other large estates in the vicinity were owned by the late Walter Strong, onetime publisher of *The Daily News*, and the late Medill McCormick, former owner of the *Chicago Tribune* and United States Senator.

In Lilacia Park

EACH YEAR, in late April or early May, several thousand visitors come to Lombard, attractive residential village some twenty miles west of Chicago, to witness the village's annual Lilac Festival. This colorful, fragrant, springtime event is to Illinois what the Blossom Festival is to Michigan or the Cotton Festival to Tennessee. When it is being held, and the trim, green lawns of Lombard are enchanting with purple, blue, red, and lavender lilacs, motorists from all directions may be seen converging on the village's principal show place—Lilacia Park.

On a grassy knoll in this park, under a great old silver aspen, stands an ancient house that has become an object of veneration to Lombardians and to lilac-lovers throughout Illinois and the Midwest. For this was the home of the late Colonel William R. Plum, pioneer resident of the village—soldier, lawyer, traveler, writer, horticulturist, and founder of Lilacia Park. Containing more than three hundred varieties of lilacs from all parts of the world, this park is regarded by botanists as the finest lilac garden in the Western Hemisphere.

The Plum home is of frame construction, white-painted, gable-

Chicago Daily News

William R. Plum House, Lombard, Built 1869.

roofed, and with a spacious veranda across its front. It now houses Lombard's public library—the Helen W. Plum Memorial Library, named in honor of Colonel Plum's wife. A lineal descendant of Roger Williams, Helen Williams married Colonel Plum in 1867 and two years later they moved into the house which stands today as a memorial to them. It was his wife, Colonel Plum always said, who first aroused in him an interest in lilacs.

"In 1911, when we were on a tour of Europe," Colonel Plum once told a family friend, Mrs. Annabelle Seaton, "we stopped at Nancy, in France, and there visited the famous lilac gardens of Pierre La Moine. That visit proved my downfall. My wife purchased two choice lilac specimens, a double white and a double purple, and we brought them back to Lombard. From that time on my enthusiasm for lilacs grew and I have never lost interest in them since."

When Colonel Plum made this statement, the results of his hobby could be seen all about the old Plum home. Here were all types of lilacs, including one of his favorites, a blue variety called the "President Lincoln." The shrubs were pleasingly arranged on the Plum estate of two and a half acres, which he called "Lilacia." Since expanded to ten acres, Lilacia—re-named Lilacia Park—now contains 1,500 lilac bushes as well as 87,000 tulip bulbs.

Before settling in Lombard, Colonel Plum had served as an expert telegrapher in the Civil War under General George H. Thomas. He afterward went to Chicago, where he engaged in the practice of law. Then, following his marriage, he took up residence in Lombard. This was about the time that Lombard was platted as a village by Joseph Lombard, a Chicagoan. A few years later Colonel Plum served, for several terms, as village president. He and his wife were, from the beginning, leading and highly esteemed residents of the village and remained so throughout their lives.

In addition to being a lilac-grower and horticulturist, Colonel Plum was also an accomplished writer, as was his wife. Two prized volumes in the library which now occupies the Plum home are his novel, *The Sword and the Soul*, a story of the Civil War, and his *The Military Telegraph During the Civil War in the United States*, an authoritative work.

During the many years Colonel and Mrs. Plum occupied their Lombard home, the interior was comfortably furnished in the style of the 1860's, and an atmosphere of dignity and culture always prevailed. Solid walnut furniture adorned the rooms—carved chairs, old-fashioned rockers, marble-topped tables, and numerous ornamental cabinets and chests which contained Civil War relics, as well as souvenirs and trophies from all sections of the globe. The colonel's book-lined den, with its fine billiard table of inlaid woods, was on the second floor.

Colonel Plum died in 1927 at eighty-two, his wife having died a few years earlier. In his will he bequeathed his estate and house to the village, with the stipulation that the estate be converted into a park and the house into a free library as a memorial to his wife. He also left $25,000 to further this plan. An auction of his belongings, including his antique furniture and valuable law library, brought in additional funds for the establishment of the park.

The terms of Colonel Plum's will were carried out, a park commission was set up by the village board, and the services of a world-famous Chicago landscape architect, Jens Jensen, were obtained to create Lilacia Park. Tulips were added to the lilac collection. Afterward, the Lombard Lilac League was created to hold an annual lilac festival. This has been held each year since and is marked by pageantry, color, the night lighting of Lilacia Park, music, and the selection of a lilac queen—all against a fresh, bright, varicolored background of lilac blooms throughout "The Lilac Villa."

During this time, the old Plum home is as much an object of interest as the park around it. Some nine thousand volumes are housed on the shelves here. On the walls hang large portraits of Colonel and Mrs. Plum. This portion of the house has been remodeled for library purposes, but the second floor remains largely intact and contains many pieces of furniture from the Plum household.

The big silver aspen in front of the house is now known as "Mother's Tree"—so-called because it owes its existence largely to Colonel Plum's mother-in-law. The story is told that she discovered it as a sapling when her son-in-law was clearing out the underbrush around his house soon after moving into it. She prevailed on him to transplant the sapling.

"And Willie, like a dutiful son, set it out in front of the house," writes Mrs. Seaton, "where all through the years since it has grown and flourished like the legendary green bay tree, and to family and friends became known as 'Mother's Tree.'"

Standing near "Mother's Tree" is a sturdy Schwedler maple which the Plums brought back from the Black Forest in Germany. Here, also, is a Chinese ginkgo tree and a native Ohio buckeye. The center of the park is marked by a lily pool and a goldfish pond.

Over the graves of Colonel and Mrs. Plum, near Cuyahoga Falls, Ohio, stand two handsome lilac bushes—offshoots of the two original French bushes which formed the nucleus of the famous Plum collection.

Architectural Landmark

NOT REALLY an old house, although built in the 1890's, the curious, rambling, brick-and-shingle dwelling at the southeast corner of Forest and Chicago avenues in Oak Park, survives as an important landmark in the evolution of "modern," or twentieth century, domestic architecture. For this house was designed and occupied by Frank Lloyd Wright, now regarded by many as the foremost living American architect.

What makes this house especially interesting is the fact that it was built more than fifty years ago, or at a time when architecture was still in an imitative stage, copying Gothic castles, Renaissance palaces, and Romanesque strongholds. In this house we see the beginnings of Wright's unique method of design, a design that helped to bring about the rise of what the public calls "modern" architecture but which architects identify as the "international" style.

In designing his Oak Park home, Frank Lloyd Wright broke with tradition and created a dwelling whose form was determined, not by any French chateau or Viennese palace, but by its function—in this case, a place in which to live in a modern manner. It was, in fact, the first of his series of houses "designed for living." Several of these still stand on Forest Avenue, in the vicinity of the original Wright home, and have made Oak Park a mecca for architectural historians.

Frank Lloyd Wright was born on June 8, 1869, at Richland Center, Wisconsin. His father, William, was a traveling musician, who later became a preacher, and his mother, the former Anna Lloyd-Jones, was a school teacher. After attending the public schools and studying engineering at the University of Wisconsin, Wright left college without completing his courses and went to Chicago. This was in 1888, and soon he had obtained employment in the office of Adler and Sullivan, two of the city's leading architects of the 1880's and 1890's.

It was during his Adler-and-Sullivan period that Wright married Catherine Tobin, a Chicago girl, who was nineteen at the time, while he was twenty-one. And, in 1891, shortly after his marriage, Wright built his Oak Park house. In his autobiography he says that building this home was made possible by a substantial advance on his salary given him by his employer, Sullivan. In 1893 Wright left the partners to begin his career as an independent architect, a career that was to bring him world-wide fame.

In the years when they were living in their Oak Park house, a dwelling that was part home and part architect's studio, the Wrights became

209

Frank Lloyd Wright House, Oak Park, Built 1891.

the parents of six children. Some idea of what life was like in this household may be gained from Wright's autobiography, which was published in 1932. In it we learn of the children and of how the father gave them musical instruments to play, how the family owed a grocery bill of $850, and of Wright's interest in books, prints, rugs, and handicraft articles. We are told, also, of the old willow tree around which a corridor was built connecting the main part of the house with the studio.

The Wrights lived in this house for nineteen years. Then in 1911, after being divorced from his wife, Wright built a country house at Spring Green, Wisconsin, near his boyhood home, and here he has lived since. Called "Taliesin," the place has become widely known because of its architecture and as a school for architectural students.

After Wright left his Oak Park house, it was occupied for some years by his divorced wife and his children and subsequently was purchased by Alfred MacArthur, a Chicago insurance executive, patron of the arts, and friend of Wright's. Here, too, came to live MacArthur's brother, Charles, who was then a Chicago newspaperman. He afterwards became a playwright, scenario writer, husband of Helen Hayes, and collaborator with Ben Hecht in the writing of *The Front Page* and other Broadway plays and Hollywood movies.

Wright was still somewhat under the influence of conventional architecture when he designed his Oak Park house. This is evidenced by the gabled roof. He had not then achieved the flat, or low-pitched roof which marks typical Frank Lloyd Wright houses of today. Aside from the roof, however, the Oak Park house contains all of the characteristics of Wright's method of design—horizontal lines, overhanging eaves, simplicity of trim, and rows of windows.

On visiting the interior, one is surprised at the "modern" features of the rooms and that such "modernism" was created in an age of late Victorian gilt, decoration, and trim. Here, the ceilings are simple and low and leaded glass windows of plain design let in the daylight. The opening of the great brick fireplace is sunk below the floor and there is no overmantel. The house does not contain a basement. The studio, where Wright first conceived buildings that were to make architectural history, is lighted by large north and east windows.

In this house architectural students may see the latest phase of domestic architecture in Illinois during the nineteenth century, a manifestation that pointed the way to twentieth century house design. And in the same state of Illinois, as was pointed out at the beginning of this book, one may find the earliest phase of permanent shelter construction —the Saucier log house at Cahokia.

INDEX